Voice and song

To James F. Bosma, who showed that the vowel is formed in the upper pharynx, thus explaining the basic physiology of the dorsal method of singing

Voice and song

Sine Butenschøn
and
Hans M. Borchgrevink

———

CAMBRIDGE UNIVERSITY PRESS

Cambridge

London   New York   New Rochelle
Melbourne   Sydney

Published by the Press Syndicate of the University of Cambridge
The Pitt Building, Trumpington Street, Cambridge CB2 1RP
32 East 57th Street, New York, NY 10022, USA
296 Beaconsfield Parade, Middle Park, Melbourne 3206, Australia

Originally published in Norwegian as *Stemme og sang*
by Dreyer, Oslo in 1978 and © Sine Butenschøn 1977

First published in English by Cambridge University Press 1982
as *Voice and song*
© Sine Butenschøn and Hans M. Borchgrevink 1982

Printed in Great Britain at
the University Press, Cambridge

Library of Congress catalogue card number: 81-38464

British Library Cataloguing in Publication Data
Butenschøn, Sine
Voice and song.
1. Singing
I. Title II. Stemme og sang. *English.*
784.9   MT893

ISBN 0 521 28011 7

Contents

Preface

In 1973 Sine Butenschøn, an experienced teacher of voice and singing technique, was preparing an essay on the anatomical and physiological basis of the 'dorsal method of singing'. She consulted Hans M. Borchgrevink, MD and musician, Fellow of the Norwegian Research Council for Science and the Humanities, for his advice on the English translation of the essay. Borchgrevink thought it would be more appropriate to present the material in an expanded version addressed to the student and teacher of singing. This book is thus the result of collaboration between an experienced teacher and a scientifically educated student of singing.

Singing is taught by means of a language of symbols and fantasy which expresses the teacher's subjective perceptions of singing. The aim of this book is to explain to teacher and student what bodily functions this language sets in motion. The act of singing involves the body in a great many different ways. Correct singing technique demands a controlled use of the entire body, and intimate knowledge and understanding of the physiological processes involved will ensure a profound insight into the mechanisms of voice production. Unfortunately, medico-scientific research has mostly neglected the problems posed by singing. However, where appropriate studies exist, the explanations given are based on objective scientific data from publications on anatomy, physiology and phonetics. Other mechanisms are explained by referring to Sine Butenschøn's experience of the subjective perceptions evoked in the singer and/or the characteristics and signs that can be observed by the teacher.

We have attempted to present the material in a concise form and in a way that requires no special prior knowledge on the part of the reader. We have chosen an approach where scientific explanations are presented side by side with pedagogical instructions. Thus we hope that the scientific data can be linked to well-known subjective experiences in the singer.

The basis of the presentation is a method that has been called 'the dorsal method' because, when breathing, and particularly in the pitching and maintenance of a note, it produces effects that are especially felt in the dorsal region. We should emphasise that this method is not to be considered the only correct one; but we hope experienced singers will discover points of similarity with their own method, and, no matter which method they themselves prefer, they should benefit from the scientific information presented. The dorsal method represents Sine Butenschøn's system of evoking awareness and control of the singing function in accordance with the physiological processes which we have here endeavoured to explain. However, an important aim of the book is to deal with the mechanics of voice and song production so thoroughly as to provide a basis for fruitful discussion of concrete features in an otherwise diffuse subject.

S.B.
H.M.B.

How to use this book

This book is addressed to the singer, the student of singing and the singing teacher as well as to speech and music therapists and to all medical staff dealing with the problems of singers. It can be used in private study, as an aid to teaching, or as a work of reference relating to the voice, voice production and to singing.

In addition it is recommended that the student follow certain clearly defined procedures. Start every lesson by singing through all the vowels. This applies to all students *regardless* of level. Spoken vowels differ from vowels in singing (see chapter 1) and consequently everyday speech leads to the degeneration of the sung vowel. Train your ear to recognise the correctly sung, 'full-bodied' vowel sound.

Level 1 (beginner). The untrained student should begin by humming a note (see exercises 1—4) and practising *only* vowels until they are reasonably well sung. Details are given in the exercises in this book. Start with your favourite vowel and then repeat the exercise on all the vowels in turn.

Level 2. Sing the vowel progression of simple short songs (nursery rhymes, Christmas carols), i.e. omit the consonants from the words, but preserve the proper rhythm and intonation.

Level 3. Sing the words of the tune as if they were an unbroken chain of vowels, shifting directly from one vowel to the next whilst 'putting the consonants in between'. Preserve the proper rhythm and intonation.

Level 4. The difficulty of melody, rhythm, intonation and interpretation in the songs should be increased progressively.

Note: Every lesson should start with singing through all the vowels. All singers should receive regular control and correction by their singing teacher as bad habits are easily acquired.

1

Speech versus song

In principle there is no difference between the sounds of speech and of singing. However, in singing the consonants should not break the flow of vocal sound in the same way as in speech. The extent to which the speaking voice is 'sonorous' depends on the intensity given to the vowel within each syllable. (A syllable consists of a vowel or diphthong generally combined with one or several consonants.) Singing demands considerable resonance and articulation, and for this reason is extremely useful when teaching people to improve their speaking voice.

In speech, vowel and consonant interact (see fig. 1). The tongue does not completely shape itself for the vowel but retains aspects of the consonant throughout the syllable. This incompleteness of vowel is characteristic of speech. In rapid speech consonants tend to be increasingly dominant.

In singing, the words are presented artificially, because the composer dictates the pitch and duration of the notes. Under such circumstances the vowel dominates the consonant since only it

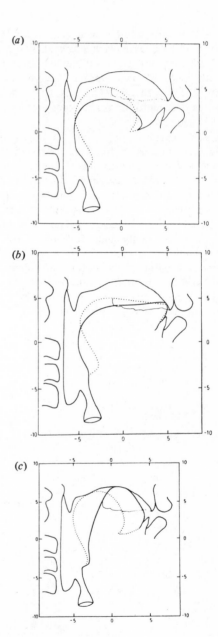

Fig. 1. Contours of the vocal tract when vowels and consonants are spoken.

(*a*) The vowels *a* [ɑ] and Swedish *u* [uː] being pronounced (continuous and dotted line respectively).

(*b*) The tip of the tongue articulating *d* as in *ada* [ɑdɑ] and Swedish *udu* [udu] (continuous line and dotted line respectively). The *d* affects the shape of the vowel. Both the raising of the blade of the tongue (the top: see fig. 25, p. 39) against the palate and the backward movement of the tongue towards the wall of the pharynx are reduced.

(*c*) Articulating *g* between two similar vowels as in *igi* [ɪgɪ] and *ugu* [ugu] (continuous line and dotted line respectively). Note that the contact between the dorsum of the tongue (the back: see fig. 25, p. 39) and the palate does not occur at the same spot. The two vowels determine the resonance in the vocal tract and thereby give colour to the consonant. (After S. Øhman (1967). *J. Acoust. Soc. Am.* **41**.)

can be sustained and developed, and therefore projected far better acoustically.

Comparison of vowels in speech and song

Long/short vowels

In speech   The long vowel in speech has a relatively long duration, and can therefore be shaped more completely (see above). In this way, two separate vowel sounds have come into existence for each intended one: the long, distinct vowel sound, and the short, indistinct vowel sound. For example, a long *u* has more *u* 'qualities' than a short *u* (e.g. *crude* as opposed to *bush*).

The short vowel is firmly established in the Germanic languages, and is here to stay. Substituting a long for a short vowel sound will entirely change the meaning of a word, as in *neat/knit* or *reach/rich*.

In song   In singing an awkward situation often arises when the performer is asked to sing a long note on a short vowel sound; on occasions it may even be necessary to change notes on the same short vowel sound. As this distorts the length of the vowel, it is important not to lose the original quality and character of the short vowel sound, otherwise the word will not be understood.

Stressed/unstressed vowels

In speech   In speech the vowel has four characteristics: volume, pitch, inflection and duration. A stressed vowel either increases in volume and then decreases, or starts at full volume, in which case the stress will be more extreme. The vowel may change pitch, gliding upwards or downwards or rising and falling: the more it varies in itself the stronger the stress will be. A stressed vowel is of relatively long duration.

An unstressed vowel is invariable in its volume and inflection, is of relatively short duration, and, being a short vowel, is characterised by a blurred or indistinct form. A long vowel in an unstressed position is also blurred. The opening lines of Shakespeare's *The Merchant of Venice* illustrates this point:

In sooth Ĭ knōw nŏt why Ĭ am sŏ sad

The vowels in the words 'in' and 'so' are both unstressed and therefore blurred or relatively indistinct.

In song   As in speech, vowel stress in song is produced by means of a *crescendo/decrescendo*, and in the case of strong stress the vowel has to be started full volume. However, pitch is determined by the melody, and length by the value of the note.

The volume of an unstressed vowel is stable. It is possible to sing several notes on the same unstressed vowel. However, whereas in speech a long vowel sound is blurred in an unstressed position, in song it must be distinct in the unstressed position too. This is an important factor in clear enunciation of the words in singing.

For the execution of stressed/unstressed vowels in singing, see chapter 8, p. 42.

2

Formation of voiced sounds

General survey

The site of voice production is the larynx (Adam's apple). This is situated at the top of the trachea (windpipe), and functions also to close off the entrance to the trachea (e.g. during swallowing, to prevent food entering the lungs). The part of the larynx responsible for voice production is the glottis, which contains two sets of vocal cords: the false vocal cords, and the true vocal cords (or more correctly vocal folds: see fig. 29).[1] A more detailed description of the physiology of the larynx is given in appendix 3.[2]

Vocal sound is formed when air pressure in the lungs overcomes the closing force of the vocal cords, and air is released. When pressure in the lungs decreases, the vocal folds are sucked together again, and when it rises again the whole process is repeated. This results in vibration of the exhaled air. The pitch of a note is a function of the number of vibrations per second, and is determined by the air pressure in the lungs and the thickness, tension and length of the vocal folds. For

example, the note a' has 440 vibrations, or cycles, per second (abbreviated to c.p.s.).[3]

Methods of breathing

Many muscles are used in breathing (respiration), but the main ones are the intercostal muscles between the ribs (fig. 2), and the diaphragm (fig. 3). In addition some of the throat and shoulder muscles may exert some influence on breathing. For this reason there are various types of breathing (see appendix 4).

The various methods of singing are characterised by the degree of opening of the jaw, the shaping of the lips, the singing posture and, most importantly, the method of breathing. For instance, it is possible to prepare for singing by inhaling (drawing breath), and then singing the note while exhaling (breathing out). Alternatively, the singer can follow the basic principle of the dorsal method: that the tone is not prepared by ordinary inhalation, nor formed by ordinary exhalation.

In the dorsal method the tone is prepared by means of a yawn/stretch, i.e. yawning while at the same time stretching the vertebral column (backbone). This sets in motion various reflex systems which result in air passing into the lungs. Singing is brought about by conscious use of the muscles in the back, which gives the thorax (chest) a broader and flatter shape, while the sternum (breastbone) recedes.

---

1 The vocal cord anatomically is restricted to the connective tissue margin (the vocal ligament) of the vocal fold. The vocal fold anatomically consists of the vocalis muscle plus the elastic membrane, its connective tissue margin plus the mucous membrane lining the larynx. In less precise non-medical language vocal cord is often used when vocal fold is meant. In this book the anatomical distinction between vocal fold and vocal cord will be made.

2 According to Negus the original function of the glottis was not to produce voiced sounds. Practically any throat can phonate, even without vocal cords. Species with movable upper ribs, and with the habit of independent use of the forelimbs for purposes other than locomotion, need a double valve. Air must be prevented from flowing into the lungs when the animal hangs by the arms or swings from branch to branch. In addition the thorax must be stabilised, so that more delicate motor tasks can be carried out. This, in Negus's opinion, is the origin of the vocal folds, which are especially developed in man (Negus, 1929, pp. 239–50; and 1949, p. 102).

3 In the convention used in this book for naming pitches in a specific octave (the Helmholtz system), each octave is regarded as beginning at C and rising to B. The octaves are designated in ascending order C,–B, C–B c–b c'–b' c"–b" etc., with c' = middle C.

The thorax is more or less cylindrical in shape. Its volume is greatest when its cross-section constitutes a circular disc and decreases as the cross-section becomes more ellipsoid, as it does by conscious use of muscles in the back. This decrease in volume causes the pressure of the air in the lungs to increase (pressure is inversely related to volume) and results in a current of air passing out of the lungs while the yawn (the inhalation impulse) is maintained. The current of air therefore starts *without conscious exhalation*: the current of air passing out of the lungs while the inhalation impulse is maintained is the key to control of breath. The singer needs to adopt a specific posture for this method of breathing (see fig. 8, p. 13).

Practical performance: the dorsal method

Preparing the tone

In principle the tone is formed in two stages: it is prepared and then immediately sung. Preparation of the tone takes place in the upper pharynx (see fig. 5). This can be found approximately on an imaginary line running between the ears (external auditory canals), and it is here that the 'yawn muscle' (the upper pharyngeal constrictor) is situated (fig. 27, p. 49). Generally a yawn takes place as an adjunct to breathing, i.e. at the same time as an inhalation, but the kind of yawn we are aiming at can be achieved without drawing breath. When the upper pharyngeal constrictor is tensed, reflexes pass to the diaphragm, which is lowered (see p. 53), with the result that air flows into the lungs. If the thoracic portion of the vertebral column is relieved of the body weight, we can 'play' with the back and the ribs, so that the lungs are extended downwards and backwards (dorsally).

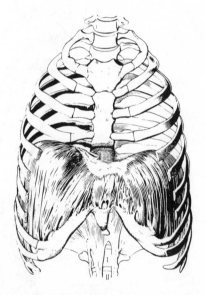

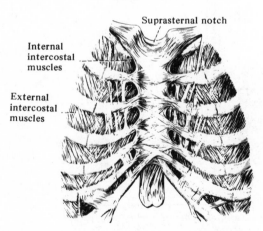

Fig. 2. The intercostal muscles fill up the spaces between the ribs, forming two oblique and intersecting layers. The outer (external) layer comprises the muscles used in inhalation (breathing in), which have fibres running obliquely down from the back to the front. When the muscles are tensed and shortened, they raise the rib below, and the thorax (chest) is thus distended. (After Benninghoff-Goerttler, 1968.)

Fig. 3. The diaphragm divides the body cavity into the thoracic cavity (chest cavity) and the abdominal cavity. It is attached to the entire lower aperture of the thorax, and rises up into the thorax in a dome shape, with muscle fibres converging from all directions in a network of ligaments at the top of the dome. The sides of the diaphragm are strongest, and here the dome rises steeply, adhering by suction to the internal walls of the thorax. The flat, sternal portion of the diaphragm takes little active part in the process of breathing.

When the diaphragm is contracted during inhalation, the dome is lowered, and the thoracic cavity is expanded. The viscera (contents of the abdominal cavity) cannot decrease in volume: they are pressed against the ribs and the abdominal wall, which yield to the pressure and are pushed out. (After Benninghoff-Goerttler, 1968.)

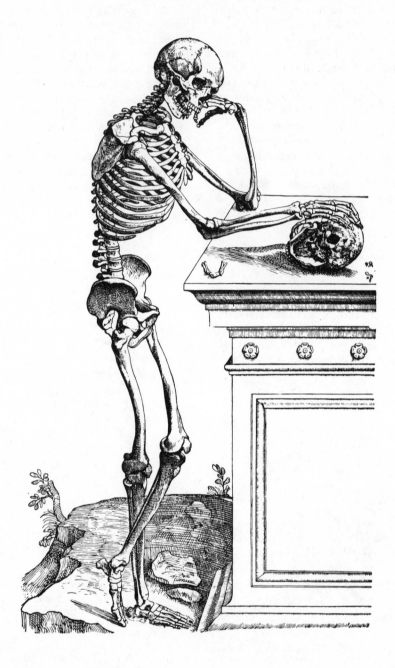

Fig. 4. The human skeleton. Note the thorax and the twelve ribs: the seven 'true' ribs extend as far as the sternum; the three 'false' ribs form the rib arches, each rib being shorter than the one above and attached to it; the two 'floating' ribs serve as insertions for muscles, and are functionally part of the abdominal wall. The five lumbar vertebrae (i.e. those below the ribs) and the pelvis with the hip-joint are also shown.

Exercise 1. How to sit

Sit on a chair. Do not lean back; let your body tilt forward slightly without stooping. (Keep this position for exercises 2 to 6 as well.) Place the four fingertips of one hand on the front of your throat, horizontally, with index finger uppermost and all the fingers slightly flexed. Breathe in: the larynx will remain motionless. Yawn: if the larynx slips down under your fingers, this is proof that the upper pharyngeal constrictor is correctly activated (see p. 48).

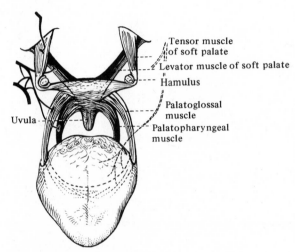

Fig. 5. The upper pharynx. The upper portion of the pharynx is concealed by the soft palate (velum palatinum). It contains two pairs of muscles, both attached to the side walls of the upper pharynx. The levator (lifter) muscle of the soft palate runs obliquely from here forwards and down, and is anchored at the other end to the roof of the palate. This pencil-thin muscle pulls the palate up and back, producing a large oral cavity. The tensor muscle of the soft palate originates just in front of the levator and its vertical portion terminates in a tendon that makes a right-angled turn round the hamulus. This is a bony protrusion that can be felt with the finger at the side of the palate, on a level with the backmost molar. Some of the descending muscles of the pharynx originate from the horizontal portion of the tensor.

The horizontal part of the tongue is also shown, stretching as far back as the point where it curves back and down into the pharynx. There are two palatal arches, the further back of which consists of the palatopharyngeal (soft-palate-to-pharynx) muscle, which is embedded in the back of the pharyngeal wall. The tonsils are situated between the two palatal arches.

The uvula in man is the vestigial remains of a longer palate (Negus, 1949, p. 25). It has no function or significance in voice production. (After Benninghoff-Goerttler, 1967).

The yawn/stretch

As the singer yawns in the way that has been described above, the vertebral column must also be stretched: this may be called the song-stretch. The stretch demands a balanced poise, which depends mainly on the inclination of the pelvis (see p. 00). Stretching in the usual sense of the word is brought about by tensing the muscles at the back of the vertebral column (the erector spinae muscle: fig. 7). But our objective is to release the head, which should be held erect, without restraint either in the nape of the neck or under the chin. To do this the cervical column (the vertebral column in the neck) is straightened, producing a characteristic posture with a slight forward lean (see fig. 8, p. 13, and fig. 22, p. 35).

Exercise 2. How to stretch

First, place an index finger on the 'nodding joint' (at the back of the head between the base of the skull and the top of the vertebral column) and push it upwards. Your head will make a very tiny nod if the joint is properly relaxed. Then find the mastoid process on each side of the skull (just behind the ears: see fig. 10, p. 19). With both index fingers pressed beneath the mastoid processes, push your head upwards. When this is done correctly (in a very relaxed way with a tiny nod) the cervical column will straighten out, tilting the face slightly downwards.

During the yawn/stretch the segments[4] of the thorax, one below the other, are then brought into play in the stretch (see exercise 5).[5]

Mistake no. 1. Pulling down the back of the head, so that the face tilts up. This is caused by tensing the muscles at the back of the cervical column.

Mistake no. 2. The opposite of the above: the chin is actively pulled in, resulting in a double chin.

---

4 Primitive animals, e.g. the earthworm, can clearly be seen to consist of discs or segments. In man the vertebrae, the ribs and the muscles between the ribs are specialised parts of similar primaeval segments.
5 As a teacher, one of the authors (S.B.) has come across problems for which the available literature has been unable to provide an explanation. In such cases Professor Johan Torgersen of the Anatomical Institute of Oslo University was asked whether her hypotheses in such cases were *possible* solutions from an *anatomical* point of view. Where the answer was in the affirmative, he is referred to in the text. The question was not whether the hypothesis was *correct* from a pedagogical point of view.

Covering the tone

Covering the tone in singing takes place automatically when the yawn is carried out correctly. When the tone is covered, the opening of the jaws increases, and the dorsum (back) of the tongue slides back (see fig. 19, p. 32). When the larynx is lowered in yawning (exercise 1), it carries with it the hyoid bone, to which the root of the tongue is attached (fig. 28, p. 50). The root of the tongue is therefore lowered, while the dorsum slides back (fig. 25, p. 39), which should leave a clear passage right down into the lungs.

Exercise 3. The yawn/stretch

Sit correctly and calmly. Yawn and simultaneously stretch the vertebral column. As yawning implies a reflex lowering of the diaphragm, air will naturally flow into the lungs. Don't 'take' a breath!

3

Humming the tone

Humming is simply singing without vowels. The mouth is closed, and the sound passes through the nose. Humming limits the yawn, but not the stretch. Timbre and stretch can be experienced distinctly by the singer when humming.

Resonance

Humming gives a special perception of resonance: a 'resonance cavity' can be felt to exist behind the soft palate, whenever, as in singing with the use of a yawn, the pitch is 'drawn up' and the cervical column simultaneously stretched. The pitch cannot, of course, literally be 'drawn up', as it consists of sound waves spreading towards the place of exit of the air from the body (the nose in the case of the hummed note and the mouth in the case of the sung note). The feeling of a resonance cavity is due to the operation of the upper pharyngeal constrictor muscle, which relates directly to the diaphragm. The more highly trained the singer, the greater the consciousness of the interplay between the upper pharynx and the diaphragm (provided of course that a correct singing posture is maintained).

Exercise 4. Perception of resonance

With teeth apart hum *m*, *n* or *ng*, making sure that your lower jaw is 'hanging from your cheeks' (fig. 10, p. 19). Feel for the resonance cavity behind the soft palate.

Exercise 5. Perception of stretch

Hum a note anywhere in the register between b and b' flat,[6] as shown. Feel the yawn/stretch

6 The pitch indicated refers throughout to women's voices. The male voice would be pitched an octave lower.

'draw the sound up' into the resonance cavity, which is felt to be in the very centre of the head. Let the dorsal area (back) of the thorax expand, so that it fills out as the sound is 'sucked in'; the precise extent to which the sound is 'sucked in' depends on the pitch sung. The expansion must come from inside, from the area between the ribs and the diaphragm, without assistance from the shoulders and arms.

Hum a low note, and then let is slide upwards, like a siren. More and more 'segments' of the back become involved as the air pressure in the lungs increases, so that you feel as though the sound originates from ever lower down the vertebral column as the pitch slides up. Every pitch has its own special place of origin; the higher the note the lower the level in the vertebral column where it is formed. A low pitch is felt to expand 'under the yoke', i.e. beneath the shoulders, whilst a high pitch expands further down in the vertebral column.

The support area

The support area is to be found in the lower portion of the abdominal wall (fig. 6). Here the three broad abdominal muscles run almost parallel, enabling the abdominal wall to be drawn up and in without the rib-cage being drawn down into the exhalatory position at the same time (Benninghoff-Goerttler, 1968, p. 237).

Exercise 6. Perception of the support area

Sit down and place one hand on your lap with its palm against the abdominal wall. Say an emotional 'no' as loudly as you can. The tone seems to be sucked up from the depths of the body. Feel a jerk from the support area along the edge of your little finger, i.e. from the very bottom of your abdomen. What is happening is that the abdominal wall is tensed, so that the viscera, the contents of the abdominal cavity, are forced up against the lowered diaphragm thereby increasing the air pressure in the lungs. In singers' language this is called 'supporting the tone'. Different methods of singing use different techniques for creating this support.

When the glottis is open (i.e. when the vocal cords are apart), the abdominal wall acts as the true exhalatory muscle. When the glottis is closed, the tensed abdominal wall functions to increase the pressure in the abdominal cavity, for instance when the bowels are emptied or when giving birth.

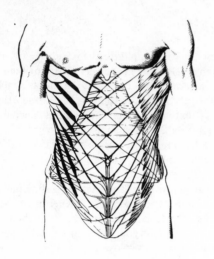

Fig. 6. The abdominal wall: the directions of pull of the broad abdominal muscles. The abdominal wall consists of several layers of muscle connecting the upper edge of the pelvis with the thorax. Three broad, flat, thin layers of muscle run from behind, encircling the sides of the body, and extending as far as the vertical rectus muscle in the middle of the abdominal wall, as follows: (1) the transverse muscle of the abdomen forms a transverse band which is covered by (2) the internal oblique abdominal muscle, which in turn is covered by (3) the external oblique abdominal muscle. (After Benninghoff-Goerttler, 1968.)

4

Poise and stance: singing posture

So far you have been asked to sit whilst singing. Standing erect is no easy matter: we do not *retain* our balance, but are always busy *regaining* it. The beginner is therefore recommended to sit (correctly) through his lessons until he has reached a certain level of proficiency.

Good poise means the balanced position that involves the least possible tension of the two groups of muscles shown in fig. 7. Their relative tension determines the inclination of the pelvis. However, there is a distinction between poise and working position, in this case the singing posture. Poise is the position the various parts of the body assume in relation to one another in a normal standing position (Alvik, 1953), whilst a working position is the adaptation of this poise which aligns the body favourably for the work to be carried out.

The dorsal method is based on the reflex actions of the muscles attached to the ventral (front) side of the vertebral column (as opposed to the tensing of the erector spinae muscle, which is attached to its dorsal side). As such reflex actions cannot take place if the muscles are tensed for other reasons, they must not play an active part in maintaining the poise. Consequently, the singing posture must be erect and well balanced, with the necessary degree of pelvic inclination.

Mistake no. 1. Insufficient inclination of the pelvis causes the sternum to be lowered, so that support is provided by the pit of the stomach (epigastrium) rather than the true support area.

Mistake no. 2. Excessive inclination of the pelvis produces tension in the lumbar regions of the vertebral column. This prevents the support area from functioning.

A stooping stance can be corrected by re-orientating the muscles in the upper part of the vertebral column.

Exercise 7. Poise muscles

Lie on your stomach, with your arms along the sides of your body, and your face resting on a towel. Tensing the muscles round the lowest cervical vertebra (the bony protuberance at the back of the neck), raise the topmost thoracic

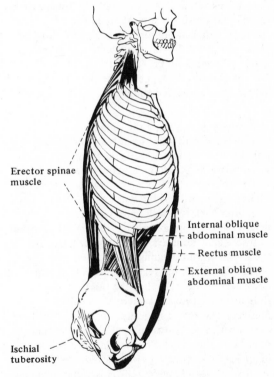

Erector spinae muscle

Internal oblique abdominal muscle

Rectus muscle

External oblique abdominal muscle

Ischial tuberosity

Fig. 7. Stance or poise muscles. The erector spinae muscle is situated on the dorsal side of the vertebral column, and tensing it thus bends the column backwards. This is counteracted by tensing the abdominal wall, especially the rectus muscle, which bends the vertebral column forwards and thus restores the balance. (After Benninghoff-Goerttler, 1968).

vertebrae (vertebrae in the chest region) and the cervical column, without pulling the head back. 'Watch your reflection' in the towel to ensure that the exercise is carried out correctly, but raise the head only slightly, without tensing the lumbar regions. It is a good idea to repeat this exercise about twenty-five times a day.

Exercise 8. Singing posture: standing (fig. 8a)
Take up an erect and relaxed standing position. Bend forwards slightly from the very bottom of the lumbar vertebrae so that the support area of the abdominal wall is ready for action. The support area will then be placed beneath the upper part of the torso, and will be flattened. Do not use the rectus muscle of the abdominal wall, as this will result in the bending of the hip-joint, and you will then find yourself out of breath. Do not arch the back either, as this will result in a lowering of the thorax. Posture is important to the quality of the tone. You can support the tone above or below the navel. The latter results in a darker, more full-bodied timbre (in German, *Vollton*). In the dorsal method support above the navel gives a lighter, less full-bodied timbre.

Exercise 9. Practising the singing posture
Concentrate first on the ankle joints. Stand upright, with straight knees, and sway backwards: when forwards the ankle joints will be flexed; when backwards the ankle joints will be stretched. The flexed position is the correct one. Now, stand with your back to a wall, with your feet half the length of your foot away from the wall. Lean your buttocks and shoulders, but not your head, against the wall. Without bending your knees, relax the tension in the lumbar regions, and flatten your body against the wall, allowing the buttocks to slide down (without the aid of the buttock muscles). Place your fingertips against the wall, on a level with your waist, and push away, so that your body stands erect but retains its position unchanged, as though set in a mould. Only the ankle joints should be flexed. This is the singing posture for the dorsal method, 'friendly, obliging and prepossessing'. Note that the abdominal wall is flattened (up and in) in the support area. The body is front-heavy and has a tendency to topple forwards. For this reason the beginner should stand behind a chair, hands resting on its back, to support the weight 'on all fours'.

Exercise 10. Sitting: the dorsal method
Do as described in fig. 8c.

Exercise 11. Humming a fifth (sitting or standing)
With a yawn/stretch, hum two notes a fifth apart, within the register b to b′ flat. Pause between the two notes. Notice the difference in the two notes. Hum the lower note again, pause, and then increase the yawn/stretch as you hum the higher note; the crown of the head (not the face!) will reach for the ceiling. In this way the higher pitch has been produced by involving more of the 'segments' of the thorax.

Go back to the lower note. You will feel that the path of the yawn up to the resonance cavity is situated behind the corresponding path for the higher note. Using the yawn/stretch the cervical column straightens out and moves more directly back under the head. This means in effect that the head is inclined forwards *a trifle* more.

Exercise 12. Ascending glissando
Slide up the pitch, siren-like, from a low note. Pay particular attention to the song-stretch. What happened at b′ natural? Was the note still clear, or did it 'fall from the resonance cavity and down onto the larynx'?

When the tone slides from b′ flat to b′ natural (a transition to the middle register: see below p. 36) the back is expanded in a new way, i.e. down in the waist. Now the siren tone can continue to rise, reaching e″ flat, but not e″ natural. Was there room for e″ natural in the pharynx, or did it lack resonance?

Under the upper part of the arms there is a muscle which provides lateral tension in the ribcage. This is the serratus anterior muscle (see fig. 9). Using the serratus anterior, extend the thorax laterally, out towards the arms, which should be hanging down passively. Do not raise the shoulders (as this will detract attention from the ribs) and do not inhale. This muscle gives the thorax width but has no effect on the breathing (Campbell, 1958). Check your posture. If the sternum droops, the muscle cannot obtain a hold, as the shoulder-blades will slide to the sides. The muscle will also be unable to function properly if the back is tensed.

Hum e″ flat, and then, while continuing the song-stretch and expanding the thorax, e″ natural.

12

Continue to ascend the scale.

Repeat the slide from the low note; when there is no room for the tone in the upper pharynx, expand the thorax, first in the waist and then in the sides of the body.

Exercise 13. Descending glissando
Slide the pitch of the note down from the high register. Feel the support pressing the viscera against the diaphragm. As the pitch drops, this pressure will be felt deeper and deeper in the abdominal cavity, provided that the small of the back is relaxed and the singing posture correct. The yawn, too, can be felt to move inwards, and 'the note is sucked higher up into the head'.[7] In other words, when the sequence of notes is descending, the support pressure and the yawn/stretch both move inwards/upwards.

Fig. 8. Singing postures.
(*a*) Standing, dorsal method (exercise 8). See the section on preparing the tone (p. 5) and the yawn/stretch (p. 7). The curvatures of the vertebral column in the cervical and lumbar regions are straightened out; the face is *not* turned up.

(*b*) Standing, a ventral method. The chin is raised, and the thoracic vertebrae are pressed forward and pressed into the rib-cage. The sternum is raised but the distance between the vertebral column and the sternum is shortened: the thorax is flattened, and its volume decreases the higher the pitch.

7 This is not so in actual fact: the soft palate assumes a lower position on the deep note than on the high. The sensation must be due to other causes.

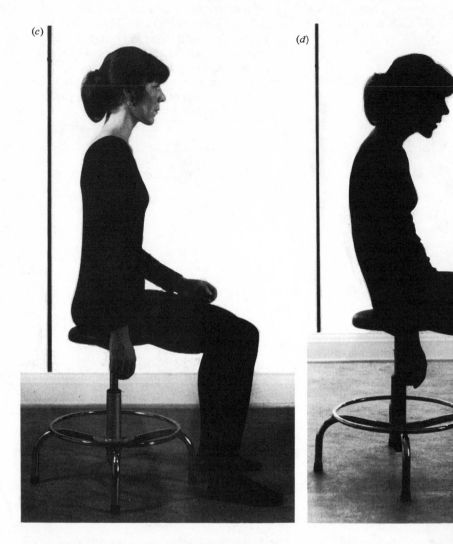

(c) Sitting, dorsal method. Sit down, making sure that the stool (or chair) is the right height, so that your feet are resting on the floor, and the knees are bent at right-angles, while the thighs are resting on the seat or the stool or chair. Bend at the hip-joint, rather like a clasp-knife, and sit *fully* into the seat. We have four support points: the two ischial tuberosities (see figs. 7 and 11) and the thighs. 'Sit on your thighs.' The upper part of the body should be inclined forwards sufficiently to ensure this. You should experience a sense of contact with your support area. (In the standing and supine position the tuberosities of the ischium are covered by the gluteus maximus muscle. In the upright sitting position of the dorsal method the muscle slides up, and the tuberosities are uncovered.)

(d) How *not* to sit. If you sit forwards on the seat, allowing your back to slip backwards, the pelvis will follow and will also tip backwards. The thorax will then sink and flatten out, and the head will compensate for this by craning forwards, resulting in a meagre tone.

14

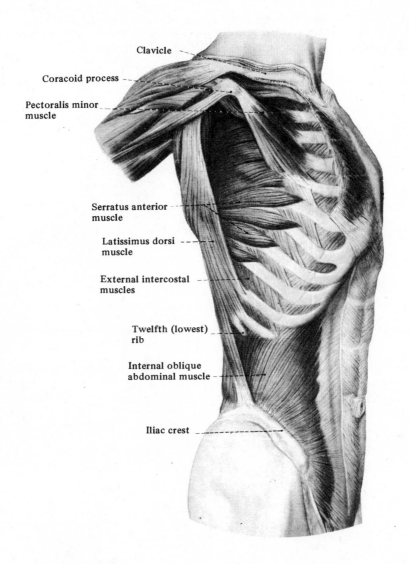

Clavicle

Coracoid process

Pectoralis minor
muscle

Serratus anterior
muscle

Latissimus dorsi
muscle

External intercostal
muscles

Twelfth (lowest)
rib

Internal oblique
abdominal muscle

Iliac crest

Fig. 9. The serratus anterior muscle and the pectoralis minor muscle.

The serratus anterior originates on the vertebral margin of the shoulder-blade, running forwards between the shoulder-blade and the thorax; its other end is attached to the sides of the nine uppermost ribs. When the muscle is tensed and the shoulder-blades are held still, the shape and suspension of the ribs will cause the thorax to be expanded (broad and flat).

The pectoralis minor muscle is attached at one end to the coracoid process, a hook-like projection that curves from the shoulder-blade forwards across the shoulder joint. The muscle then slopes forwards and down, the other end being attached to the third, fourth and fifth ribs, close to the side of the sternum. It is active when singing in the very low register. (After Benninghoff-Goerttler, 1968.)

Descending from b' flat, the point of attack in the cervical column descends, reaching the lowest cervical vertebra at b natural and the topmost thoracic vertebra at b flat. This is what is meant by the yawn 'moving in'. Simultaneously there is a corresponding lower thoracic point of attack which is felt to move upwards. If this exercise is performed correctly you will feel the head 'rise' while it is tilted slightly forwards (cf. exercise 2).

'Pull the head upwards', do *not* bend forwards. What is really taking place is the contraction of the ventral muscles of the cervical column.

Mistakes. The untrained singer will tend to allow the cervical column to move *forwards* from the nape of the neck, and will attempt in this position to pull the rest of the vertebral column upwards. He will not succeed because the cervical vertebrae then 'lose contact' with the rest of the vertebral column.

5

Uttering the vowel

Acoustic articulation

The voice originates in the glottis (Fant, 1960), and it is articulated and formed in the vocal tract, which is the region from the vocal cords to the lips and nostrils. The vocal tract consists of two cavities: the pharyngeal cavity and the oral cavity. The narrow opening between the tongue and palate is referred to as the neck of the pharyngeal cavity. The neck of the oral cavity is the actual oral aperture (i.e. the jaw and lips). Both cavities and necks are of equal importance when articulating, and their interaction gives each vowel its characteristic sound.

Formants

The glottis note is the fundamental note. In addition to this a number of overtones are formed. The vocal tract can be shaped in such a way that certain pitch areas are selected and emphasised, while others are muffled or filtered away. This makes possible the production of an almost unlimited range of different sound qualities. 'Formants' are strengthened or emphasised pitch areas which give speech sounds their characteristic resonance colour. They are described as F1, F2, etc., in the same sequence as their pitch moves away from that of the fundamental note. The volume of the formants decreases in the same order, so that the first two formants, with in exceptional cases F3, are sufficient to describe the vowel sound. The first three formants can be varied at will, and independently of one another, by means of interplay between the cavities and necks in the vocal tract. If the larynx is lowered, another resonance chamber, the piriform recess, is added to the vocal tract just above the larynx. This cuts out overtones with frequencies above 5000 cycles per second (Fant, 1960), which means that

the voice does not acquire the sharp timbre caused by these high pitches.

Individual features of voice timbre

The voice of the soprano or tenor is light in resonance, while that of the alto or bass is relatively dark in timbre and resonance. This is because the anatomy differs in such a way that the strengthened overtones have a relatively high or low frequency. In addition, every voice has an individual character, dependent on the singer's technique and the individual anatomical variations. The singer can also colour the voice, making it darker by extending and lengthening the vocal tract (see above).

Extension of the pharynx

The larynx of a new-born child, like that of an animal, is situated high up. From this position it gradually sinks, till in the adult it has sunk down the distance of one or two cervical vertebrae. The pharynx is correspondingly extended, mainly in its upper part (Bosma and Fletcher, 1962). The new-born child can only move its tongue and jaw as a single unit, but when the larynx has slid down they can be moved independently (Bosma, 1963), making clear articulation possible.

The five 'articulators' of the vowel

The dorsal method involves as many as five 'articulators': jaw, lips and tongue are used for both vowel and consonant, while the upper pharynx and the shape of the thorax influence the vowel only.

English vowels, as any foreign student knows to his chagrin, are seldom pronounced in the same way as the corresponding vowels in other European languages, for instance German and Italian. English spelling in fact is not phonetic. For this reason phonetic symbols will be used to assist in identifying the English vowels (table 1).

Handholds

In order to achieve satisfactory resonance the articulation of the vowel in singing must be executed in a different manner from that of ordinary speech. This produces unaccustomed movements of the jaw, lips and tongue, so the vowels need to be practised with the aid of handholds. Handhold no. 1 puts the lips out of action, handhold no. 2 frees the jaw, and handhold no. 3 encourages the lips to be more active than in ordinary speech. All these handholds will free the jaw and give the articulators, including the upper pharynx and the thorax, greater freedom of movement.

The right and left sides of the body are seldom equally active. Use the hand from the least active side for the handholds. If the head habitually tilts to one side, restore the balance by using the opposite hand. The hand should be raised to the face, not the face lowered or turned to the hand.

At the same time as the vocal apparatus is trained, your ear must be trained to perceive your own vocal resonance and articulation. We do not hear our own voice in the same way as we hear the voices of others, because it reaches the inner ear mainly by conduction through bones in the head while the sound of other people's voices comes via the outer ear. One's own voice can be judged only in relation to itself: as to whether it is louder, softer, brighter or more resonant than it was previously. Handholds need to be used for a long time. Do not trust the untrained ear.

Exercise 14. Handhold no. 1
The vowels to be pronounced are [ɑ], [a], [ɛ], [e], [i] and the unstressed [ə]. Rest your chin in the hollow of the hand you have decided to use, and open your mouth. Using the thumb and index finger, press your cheeks in between your teeth at the position of the next-to-back tooth. This handhold will not prevent your jaw

Table 1. *Phonetic symbols for vowels*

[ɑ]	as in c*a*r
[ʌ]	as in c*u*t
[ɔ]	as in s*a*w
[ɒ]	as in h*o*t ('short [ɔ]')
[ʊ]	as in f*oo*t ('short [u]')
[u]	as in f*oo*d
[a]	as in c*a*t
[ɜ]	as in b*i*rd
[ə]	as in *a*nother
[ɛ]	as in b*e*d
[i]	as in s*ea*t
[ɪ]	as in b*i*d
[e]	as in m*a*de

from closing or being pushed forwards, but if the teeth close wrongly, your fingers will register this and help to obtain the correct opening of the jaw. Use a mirror.

Perception of the distance between the upper and lower jaws is usually rather underdeveloped (Ringel, Saxman and Brooks, 1967), and time is required to make the singer aware of the opening of the jaw.

Compensatory articulation

The broad front vowels, which are [i], [e] and [ɛ], should be articulated in a 'compensatory' manner. This means that instead of narrowing the front part of the vocal tract near the lips, the back part, the pharynx, is widened. According to the laws of physics, this produces the same result (Fant, 1960). The advantage of compensatory articulation is that it frees the jaw, and makes it possible to lower the larynx. This eliminates the highest overtones and prevents the vowels from being strident. It is the muscles from the styloid process that expand the back of the pharynx, as well as broadening the tongue. By pushing a finger in behind the angle of the jaw (fig. 13, p. 23) these muscles can be felt to swell whenever broad vowels are articulated. As the styloid process is situated in front of the cervical column, these muscles pull the head slightly forwards.

Exercise 15. Handhold no. 2: vowels articulated in a compensatory manner (i , e and ɛ)
Fig. 18*b* shows how the styloglossus muscle is attached to the lateral margin of the tongue. Say

[ɑ]. [ɛ] and [ɪ] (remember the yawn/stretch!) and feel how the muscle's point of attack moves inwards, [ɪ] being felt right back at the level of the ear canals. Note that the jaw must drop progressively as you move from [ɑ] through [ɛ] to [ɪ].

Put your hand 'in profile', index finger vertically placed up behind the front teeth. This prevents the jaw from shutting and also from being pushed forwards. With the jaw immobilised in this position, sing [ɪ]. As the jaw cannot be closed, you are forced to produce the [ɪ] by a yawn/stretch far back in the upper pharynx. If this is performed correctly you get a feeling of 'muscular pull' inside your ears and the [ɪ] seems to be escaping through the ears. Simultaneously your head will move slightly forwards and upwards.

The vowels [e] and [ɛ] are articulated in the same manner.

Vowels sung with protruding lips

In both speech and song, muscles at the sides of the lips draw them in towards the middle. In ordinary speech it is enough that the lips be merely rounded. This is done by the contraction of the orbicularis oris, or orbicular muscle of the mouth, that 'floats' in the lips and is not attached to the skeleton. In the dorsal method of singing protruded lips are required for the vowels [ɔ] and [u]. To achieve this, muscles attached to the bones of the upper and lower law (fig. 14, p. 24) supplement the action of the orbicular muscle; the corners of the mouth are drawn together while the central part of the lips remains passive and is therefore raised and protruded, away from the teeth. The jaw is now free and can be lowered.

Exercise 16. Handhold no. 3: vowels sung with protruding lips ([ɔ] and [u])
Pinch the corners of your mouth almost together from the sides, using the thumb and middle finger, at the same time pressing the cheeks in between the teeth. Put the index finger up behind the upper lip to prevent the lip from being tensed. The lip aperture will be exaggeratedly narrow and tall (relax the nape of the neck). Sing [ɔ]. Note that the central part of the upper lip is relaxed and is raised away from the front teeth. The same applies to [u].

Mistake. Don't stretch your upper lip, as this will 'displace the mouth downwards in the face'.

Exercise 17. Handhold no. 4: all vowels, at an advanced stage
Allow your jaw to 'hang from your cheeks' (on the temporal muscle: fig. 10) and let it lie relaxed in the hollow of your hand, while the index finger and the thumb rest lightly on the cheekbones. Should the lower jaw prove resistant, stroke it downwards with the fingers, in a 'meditative' motion. (Relax your neck.) This will produce the yawn. Say the vowel. The distance between the upper and lower jaws should increase as the vowel is sounded, and will increase further as the pitch rises (fig. 13, p. 23, and see exercise 18).

Back vowels and front vowels

Back vowels: [ɑ], [ɔ]
Front vowels: [ɪ], [ɛ]
X-ray investigations have shown that the back

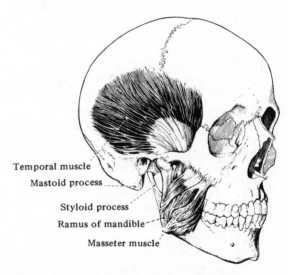

Temporal muscle
Mastoid process
Styloid process
Ramus of mandible
Masseter muscle

Fig. 10. Jaw muscles: the temporal muscle and the masseter, or chewing muscle. The temporal muscle is fastened to the coronoid process of the lower jaw (mandible) (fig. 13, p. 23), and from it the jaw hangs, with the teeth slightly parted behind closed lips. The subjective feeling is that 'the jaw hangs from the cheeks'. The masseter, or chewing muscle, is situated like a pad on the vertical part of the lower jaw (the ramus) and is tensed during chewing. (After Benninghoff-Goerttler, 1968.)

vowels are pronounced with a narrow opening of the pharynx. The vowel [ɑ] is the most characteristic (see fig. 1, nos. *a* and *c*). When pronouncing this the pharyngeal cavity is reduced to a slit between the back of the tongue and the pharyngeal wall. This constriction alone gives [ɑ] its characteristic sound. By contrast, when pronouncing the most extreme front vowel, [ɩ], the mouth is filled by the tongue and the pharyngeal cavity is open to its widest. The back vowel [ɑ] and the front vowel [ɩ], which have opposite positions for the tongue, will be dealt with first. Both are pronounced with passive lips. Handhold no. 1 and a mirror should be used.

Exercise 18. [ɑ] and [ɩ]

(1) Yawn an [ɑ] (don't say it, just yawn it) and feel how the dorsum of the tongue is drawn backwards. Yawn an [ɩ]. (Don't even whisper it, just feel what happens — and don't tense the nape of your neck.) Notice that the lower jaw (mandible) opens with a backwards pull, because the point of attack of the vowel is at the angle of the jaw (fig. 13*a*, p. 23).

(2) Pronounce [ɑ] and [ɩ] as in ordinary speech, and feel the difference. The explanation is to be found in the 'yawn muscle', the upper pharyngeal constrictor (fig. 27, p. 00). The muscle attaches to the back of the tongue (the lingual part) and to the inner border of the vertical portion of the lower jaw (the mandibular part). The lingual part works more effectively for [ɑ] (and [ɔ]), whereas the mandibular part pulls at the jaw for [ɩ] (and [e]). This method of vowel pronunciation is highly characteristic of the dorsal method of singing.

(3) Yawn, i.e. prepare the [ ] and feel how the upper pharynx forms the vowel, which should be drawn up from the support area (p. 00) using the yawn, as in exercise 1 (p. 0).

(4) Yawn [ɑ] again. Feel how the tongue slides back, so that there is only a narrow slit between itself and the back of the pharyngeal wall. The larynx is lowered. At the moment the sound is produced your back is expanded.

The front vowels [ɩ] and [e] are 'broad' vowels. The dorsum of the tongue will get broad, and the upper part of the pharynx will attain a wide shape (see below, point 6).

(5) Yawn [ɩ]. Feel the shape of the vowel in the upper pharynx. It has maximum width, and

the muscles pull it to both sides, against the ear canals.

Note: Check, by using a mirror, that the shape of the lips remains exactly the same for [ɩ] as for [ɑ]. Do not extend the lips sideways, so that the corners of the mouth are pointed as when smiling, as this will adversely affect tone quality. Do not raise the lips from the teeth as in a theatrical mask. The lower teeth should be hidden behind the lower lip.

(6) Yawn [ɩ] again. Push a couple of fingers behind the angle of the jaw (fig. 13, p. 23), and feel that the muscles from the styloid process swell when pronouncing [ɩ]. The head will move slightly forwards as the vowel is pronounced. Let the *vowel* move the head forwards — do not do it yourself. At the moment of vocalisation the tongue will achieve maximum width, the jaw will give way (fig. 19, p. 32), the yawn will lower the larynx, and the dorsum of the tongue will follow on back slightly at the moment of vocalisation, while the jaw drops accordingly. The tip of the tongue should be well forward in the mouth for all vowels.

Exercise 19. Controlling your tongue

Place an index finger on the tip of the tongue. Say [ɑ]. Note whether the tip of the tongue is jerked away. It may possibly jerk forward against the finger, just as the vowel is pronounced. If that happens then the vowel is not being 'yawned', and it 'falls down from the resonance cavity'.

Frequently novices will draw the tip into the body of the tongue, with the result that the lingual ligament and the floor of the mouth are visible.

The shape of the thorax

The use of the thorax as an articulator is a characteristic of the dorsal method. When the vowels are articulated, the dorsal muscles of the vertebral column (fig. 11) shape the thorax (J. Torgersen, personal communication).

Exercise 20. The broadening back

Feel your back getting progressively broader as the following series of sounds is sung: [ɒ] (*good*), [ɔ] (*saw*), [ɑ] (*large*), [a] (*cat*), [ɛ] (*bed*), [e] (*made*), [ɩ] (*seat*). When the broad vowels [ɩ] and [ɛ] are pronounced and the muscles of

20

the styloid process pull the head slightly forwards, the levator muscles of the ribs are simultaneously tensed (fig. 11) (J. Torgersen, personal communication). This occurs in all registers and has the effect of broadening the thorax. Not until this is done do the front vowels acquire their full width, their final perfection of form. *The lips have the same shape as for* [ɑ]. The larynx, which is now released, is also lowered. (Be sure not to push the jaw forwards! Use handhold no. 2.)

(a)

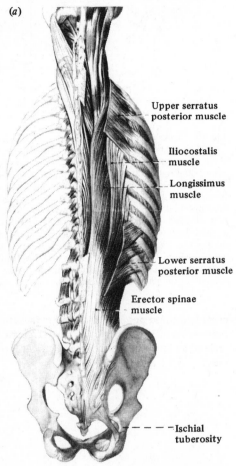

Upper serratus posterior muscle

Iliocostalis muscle

Longissimus muscle

Lower serratus posterior muscle

Erector spinae muscle

Ischial tuberosity

(b)

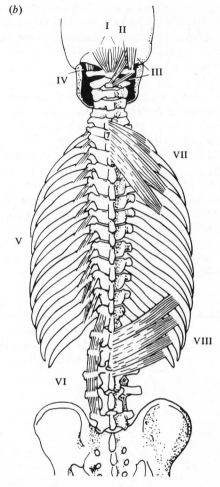

Fig. 11(*a*). The dorsal muscles, or muscles of the back (seen from the back). The upper and lower serratus posterior muscles must be consciously tensed when singing. The erector spinae muscle (see also fig. 7) is usually tensed from below, where it is attached to the hip girdle and the lower part of the vertebral column; this has the effect of straightening the back (Gray, 1977, p. 345). During the yawn/stretch, however, it operates from above, where its medial and lateral portions (the longissimus and iliocostalis muscles respectively) are attached to the thoracic vertebrae and ribs. This enables it to shape the thorax and make it work as an articulator. The levator muscles of the ribs run obliquely from the vertebrae to the rib below (see fig. 11*b*); when they are tensed the ribs are pulled upwards. (After Benninghoff-Goerttler, 1968.)

Fig. 11(*b*). I, II, III: Some muscle systems of the vertebral column (seen from the back). This group of muscles pulls the head down at the nape of the neck, turns the face up, and therefore counteracts the muscles of the ventral (front) side of the cervical column. IV: The anterior straight muscle of the head is part of the same system as the levator muscles of the ribs (see fig. 21, p. 34). V: The levator muscles of the ribs slope from the vertebra at the level of one rib to the rib beneath. VI: Muscle system V is also found between the lumbar vertebrae. VII: Upper serratus posterior muscle. VIII: Lower serratus posterior muscle. The muscles V, VII and VIII should be consciously tensed.

Exercise 21. Changing vowel

(1) Using handhold no. 2 and a mirror, say alternately the vowels [ɑ] [ɪ] [ɑ] [ɪ]. Note the change in both vowel preparation (yawn/stretch) and the shape of the thorax. The yawn shape will change the position of the tongue as you go from back vowel to front vowel and *vice versa.* (When [ɪ] is yawn/stretched the head will move slightly forwards, as described above, and you will get the *feeling* that [˙] is yawned further back than [ɑ].)

Say [ɪ]. The ribs will rise, the back will be broad. Now try [ɑ]. The yawn shape is narrower. The timbre of both vowels occurs in *the same resonance cavity*, well up behind the uvula. You will get the feeling that [ɪ] demands a greater effort than [ɑ] in order to reach right up into the cavity.

(2) The vowel [ɛ] has all the qualities of [ɪ], but to a lesser extent: it takes a wide shape in the upper pharynx and tongue, and a broad back. Say alternately [ɛ] [ɪ] [ɛ] [ɪ], and note how the shape is changed. The sound [a] (*cat*) is given a broader shape than [ɑ], without becoming as broad as [e] (*made*).

Exercise 22. [u] and [ɔ]

Both [u] and [ɔ] are back vowels. The 'pouting muscles' shape the lips (see fig. 14, p. 24). Pronounce [ɔ] and then [u]. The yawn shape in the pharynx is felt to be narrower for [u]. Repeat,

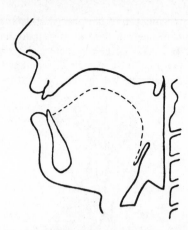

Fig. 12. The shape of the vocal tract for an unstressed [ə]. The pharynx and oral cavity together make the shape of a bent tube, but nowhere, neither between the root of the tongue and the palate, nor between the teeth and lips, is this opening narrowed. For this reason it is believed that [ə] is the slackest vowel sound in any language, and as a result it is very easy to persist in pronouncing it badly. In fact [ə], like any other vowel, has a yawn shape. For this reason it must be drawn, yawned up into the resonance cavity. If it hangs too low, breath control will be lost. Only one of the muscles from the styloid process takes part in articulating [ə]: the muscle running to the pharynx. The head is not drawn forwards.

using handhold no. 3 (p. 19), and make sure that the middle of the upper lip is raised, released and relaxed away from the teeth. Feel the difference between [ɔ] and [u].

22

6

Singing the vowel

So far we have dealt largely with exercises which *prepare* the note. You can work on these exercises as much as you like, but for short periods at a time, paying attention to yawn, stretch, yawn/stretch, dorsum of the tongue sliding back, jaw opening, upper pharynx forming the vowel, shape of thorax, singing posture, etc.

The characteristic features of the various methods of singing are, as mentioned in chapter 2: manner of breathing, posture, opening of the jaw, and the shape of the lips. In table 2 the characteristic features of the dorsal method are compared with those of a ventral method.

Preparation of the tone

As described previously, preparation of the tone in the dorsal method does not involve actively drawing breath, but a yawn/stretch, with the lower jaw 'hanging from the cheeks'; inhalation is produced by a 'gliding back' of the tongue with so little resistance that the expansion of the back is the only sign that this is taking place. A frequent mistake is to inhale positively before singing, which means that correct contact is not achieved between the upper pharynx and the support area. The yawn/stretch has not been completed and the

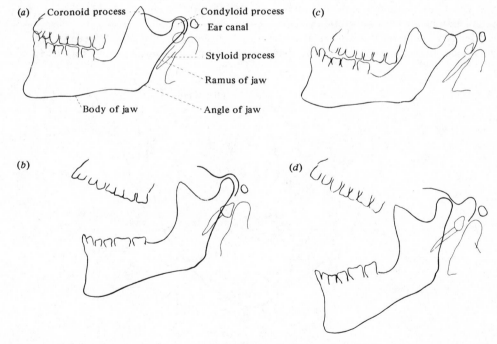

Fig. 13. The joint of the lower jaw: (*a*) closed, (*b*) opened 'hinge-like', (*c*) closed with lower jaw moving forward, (*d*) extreme opening ('dislocated')

muscles are in a position for exhalation which inhibits free interplay between them. This is immediately apparent in the vocal timbre and might be described as 'leaking tone'. The note has not been prepared 'deep enough' in the body.

Exercise 23. Singing the vowel [ɑ]

(1) Yawn/stretch the vowel [ɑ] at a certain pitch. The note will then be specifically pitched by reflex at a certain vertebral level in the back. Make sure that the pharynx retains both the [ɑ] shape and the correct *position* for preparing the anticipated pitch.

(2) Sing [ɑ]. Note that at the moment you yawn/stretch the expansion of the back produces the tone, all being elements of one action. Feel that due to the yawn, the tongue and the jaw give way and slide back. The tone sounds in the resonance cavity of the upper pharynx.

Exercise 24. A trick

'Retch' the vowel with the neck stretched and face turned down. Retching involves a tremendous expansion of the back and a violent jerk in the abdominal wall that normally causes emptying of the stomach in response to reflexes from the lower pharynx. The dorsal method of singing aims at tone production by a comparable reflex mechanism: (*a*) inhalation by reflex from the upper pharynx (yawn) to the diaphragm (Takagi, Irwin and Bosma, 1966); (*b*) tone production by reflex action from the glottis and lower pharynx to the abdominal wall, engaging the breath support (Tomori, Widdicombe and Chechoslov, 1969).

Exercise 25. Various vowels

(1) Sing the vowel [ɪ]. Use handhold no. 2 and a mirror. Note that everything broadens out in singing [ɪ] (except the lips which are, as for [ɑ], completely relaxed). The yawned [ɪ] gives the upper pharynx maximum width. The head moves forwards slightly. The tongue is subject to a lateral pull by the styloglossal muscle (figs. 15(3) and 18*b*). Feel the [ɪ] vibrating as far back as inside the ears. The dorsum of the tongue follows the lowering of the larynx, when the expanding back 'draws the vowel towards itself'. Feel the jaw being pulled open by the 'yawn muscle' (upper pharyngeal constrictor), which is attached to the angle of the lower jaw.

(2) Sing [ɛ]. It is like the [ɪ] but a little weaker in shape. Sing [ɛ] [ɪ] [ɛ] [ɪ] at the same pitch, and note the difference between the two.

(3) Sing [ɜ] (stressed [ə]). 'Draw it up towards the styloid process' (fig. 13); yawn it right up into the resonance cavity.

Exercise 26. Pausing between vowels

(1) On the same note sing [ɑ] [ɪ] [ɑ] [ɪ]

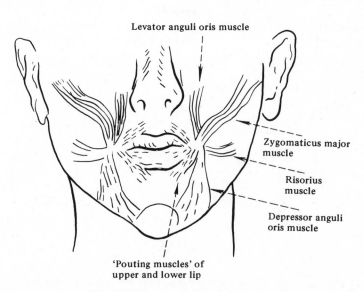

Fig. 14. Muscles radiating from the corners of the mouth.

Table 2. *A comparison of the main features of the dorsal method and a ventral method*

	The dorsal method	One of the ventral methods*
Method of breathing	Yawn/stretch for the initial note	Draw breath, inhale
Posture	Weight slightly forwards, no tension in the cervical or lower vertebral column	Upright, face lifted, sternum raised
Opening of the jaw	Moderate (fig. 13*b*)	Several variants, e.g. wide, possibly 'enormous' (fig. 13*d*)
Lips (fig. 14)	Passive, except for the vowels [ɔ] and [u], when the lips should be given a protruded shape	'Smiling lips', upper lip pressed against eye teeth

*Gardiner (1968) gives a good representation of one of the ventral methods.

with a gap between each sound. As in exercise 21 (p. 22) the yawn/stretch and the position of the head are adjusted *before* the next vowel is sung. If this is done correctly, the path taken by the [ɪ] into the resonance cavity feels further back than that taken by [ɑ]. Notice the minute change in the position of the head. For [ɑ] the entire vertebral column is stretched as a single unit, whereas for [ɪ] the pull on the vertebral column starts at the topmost joint (the 'nodding joint'), and the column is stretched from that point. In this way the [ɪ] can be yawned 'further in and higher up' in the resonance cavity. (Don't forget about the jaw 'giving way'.)

(2) Alternate [ɑ] [ɪ] [ɑ] [ɪ] but this time *legato* (i.e. with no break in resonance between vowels). Remember that each vowel must be prepared, that is, the relevant yawn/stretch must occur *before* the vowel is sung. When singing [ɪ] feel that the back broadens. Note that the shape of the lips and extent of opening of the jaw should remain unchanged.

(3) Also practise the other vowels in pairs, preferably alternating a back vowel with a front vowel (e.g. alternate *legato* [ɔ] [ɪ] [ɔ] [ɪ]).

(4) Practise all the other vowels in alternation with [ə], especially [e].

On pulmonary pressure, tone volume and jaw opening

Various measurements of lung pressure and tone volume have been made during the singing of the vowels [ɑ], [u] and [ɪ] (Faaborg-Andersen and Vennard, 1964) and it has been found that with the same lung pressure and pitch, [ɑ], which is normally sung with a wide-open mouth, is considerably stronger than [u] and [ɪ], which are normally sung with the mouth half-open. But with the dorsal method *the opening of the jaw is the same* for all three vowels ([u] being sung with protruding lips and [ɪ] being articulated in a compensatory manner: see pp. 18–19). Thus [ɑ], [u] and [ɪ] will subjectively appear equally strong, and assure a homogenous melodic line in singing. *Note*: At first one gets the *feeling* that the front vowels demand relatively greater yawn effort in order to reach all the way up into the resonance cavity.

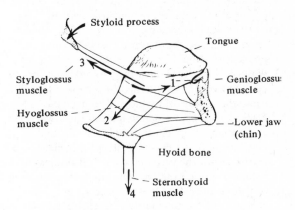

Fig. 15. The directions of pull of the external muscles of the tongue. (After Benninghoff-Goerttler, 1967.)

Changing pitch: ascending pitch

In exercise 11 (p. 12) a fifth was hummed. Now carry out the same exercise but sing instead of humming.

Exercise 27. Ascending fifth
(1) Sing an ascending fifth. Use for instance the vowel [ɔ] with handhold no. 3. Pause between the notes.

Proceed as in exercise 23 (p. 24). First yawn/stretch and sing the vowel on the pitch d′. Note the longitudinal stretch in the back of the pharynx, and be aware of the support. Then prepare the note a′. The yawn/stretch must increase – the yawn shape of the [ɔ] will be narrower and higher than for d′. In the back the point of attack as the note is prepared and pitched will have moved down, closer to the lumbar region. 'Draw from the point of attack in the back.' The dorsum of the tongue and the jaw should follow back elastically, and at the moment of realisation of the sound, the [ɔ] shape of the pharynx should be still narrower than during preparation.

Mistake. When the pitch rises it is tempting to release the shape of the vowel, so that it 'jumps out of the pharynx into the mouth'. This applies particularly to the back vowels [ɑ], [ɔ] and [u]. They will then sound more like [a] or [ə].

A given pitch can be sung with differing lengths, thicknesses and tensions of the vocal cords. The pitch will, for example, slide upwards if air pressure in the lungs is increased while the closing power of the vocal cords remains constant.

(2) Sing an ascending fifth *legato*. The vocalisation should not be disrupted between the two notes; they should be sung consecutively, *legato*. While d′ is being sounded the yawn/stretch should be increased, thus preparing the note a′. This will cause the volume of the note d′ to decrease. Expand your back when you reach the lower level appropriate for a′ and the pitch a′ will sound. Once the note has moved to its 'proper place' further down the vertebral column it regains the volume it had on the previous pitch; this regaining of volume provides a precise small accent, which is characteristic of trained singing. The secret of good coloratura singing is the presence of this accent.

Exercise 28. Singing an ascending sequence of notes legato

Starting on a note between b and d′, according to your type of voice, sing the first three notes of a scale. Move the sequence of notes up chromatically, starting each time a semitone higher than your previous starting note, until the topmost note in the sequence is b′ flat. Go back to the initial note and repeat the exercise, but this time using the first *five* ascending notes of a scale. Again, stop when the topmost note in the sequence is b′ flat. Here we are staying in the low register (see below). From the start the yawn/stretch should aim at the topmost note in the sequence. Try to get the feeling that as the pitch rises the thoracic point of attack moves further down the vertebral column. Listen critically to the vowel.

Mistake. If you do not initially aim at the topmost note, you will be stuck. It is like running over floating logs – they support you only so long as you are moving, and if you stop, the log sinks.

Transitions and registers

The expression 'transition' signifies a step on the scale at which the voice moves from one register to another. Transitions and registers are a subject much discussed by teachers of singing, but the concept has never been clearly defined. However, in practical terms the singer finds that at definite points on the scale, and in the course of a semitone step, difficulties arise which require an adjustment in the vocal apparatus.

Exercise 29. Ascending *glissando*
Sing *glissando* (i.e. sliding) upwards from your deepest note. Notice that the singing 'feels different' as the pitch rises, reaching critical points at certain levels. At one time one spoke of the 'chest register' and 'head register'. The reason for these labels was that during vocalisation the vibrating air flow gives rise to vibrations in various parts of the body depending on the pitch. In the head register the singer is conscious of vibrations in the head, for instance; the bones of the skull vibrate with frequencies as high as f‴, or 1440 cycles per second (Bekesy, 1949). The sternum (breastbone) is capable of conducting frequencies of up to c′ (261 cycles per second) or even more, depending on the

volume. In Caruso's case vibrations were registered right down to his fingertips.

Attempts have also been made to explain this phenomenon on the basis of the shape of the vocal folds. 'Full register' is then used to describe the deep notes, where the entire mass of muscle in the vocal folds participates in the vibrations, while 'marginal register' represents the high notes, where most of the muscle mass lies laterally and does not vibrate (Rubin and Hirt, 1960).

Transitions and registers in the dorsal method

Transitions to a new register occur at the same intervals on the scale irrespective of whether the pitch is going up or down, and of which vowel is being sung. The reason for this is not quite clear. The transition demands spontaneous adjustment of the thorax, the larynx, the jaw and the tongue. This must at first be done consciously, and must be practised methodically until the transitions can be mastered quite automatically.

The thorax and transitions   (For practical execution, see exercise 30, p. 29).

The three serratus muscles (upper and lower posterior, and the anterior: figs. 9 and 11) possess a particular quality, in that during singing they have to be consciously activated. They may be said to 'make the tone sound'.

In the low register (see below) the note is initiated by a yawn/stretch combined with activating only the upper serratus posterior muscle (fig. 11). In the middle register, on the 'minor transition' (see below), the lower serratus posterior muscle is also activated; and in the transition to the head register the anterior serratus muscle is activated as well (fig. 9, p. 15; exercise 12). The singer will feel the effect of the upper and lower serratus posterior muscles as an expansion of the back, while the anterior serratus muscle is felt to produce lateral extension, under the upper arm. (This assumes that the shoulder-blades are kept immobile all this time.) These actions cause the thorax to become broader and flatter, and the sternum to sink.

Fig. 9 also shows the latissimus dorsi muscle that arises partly from the three lowest ribs. At its other end it is attached to the armpit (that is to the upper end of the humerus), and when

consciously contracted it aids the transition f″ to f″ sharp.

The larynx and transitions   When a note is formed, the following take place in the larynx: (i) passive stretching of the vocal cords (vocal ligaments), (ii) active tensing of the vocal folds, and (iii) opening and closing of the glottis (see fig. 32). In addition, the larynx itself moves up and down in relation to the cervical column (fig. 17). The formation and singing of a note is the result of a complicated, but not yet clearly understood, interplay between these mechanisms. Over one hundred separate muscles or pairs of muscles control the thorax, the diaphragm, the pharyngeal resonance cavity and the glottis, and these muscles need to be adjusted very carefully and rapidly (Negus, 1957).

In the dorsal method, where great emphasis is placed on activity in the upper pharynx, details about the inside of the larynx will merely distract the singer. The following detailed description of the function of the larynx is thus included only in the interests of completeness and represents no necessary information for the successful acquisition of the dorsal method of singing. From the point of view of singing pedagogics the *position* of the larynx for varying pitches is more important than its internal structure. This position is controlled from the upper pharynx, and it is here that teaching should concentrate. The larynx is lowered when the trachea (windpipe) is exposed to a downward pull as the dome of the diaphragm is lowered during a yawn (see p. 28). In the lowered position both the vocal cords and the vocal muscles are short, thick and relaxed, resulting in low notes. If the larynx is high, the vocal cords are lengthened and the vocal muscles activated while at the same time the vibrating mass of muscle is reduced, giving rise to high notes (Sonninen, 1962). Whatever the register the rule applies that when the larynx is relatively low, the resonance is richer and more full-bodied. The vocal tract is then long, with a relatively open ventricle (fig. 29, p. 51). Furthermore, when the larynx is lowered the vocal tract acquires an extra resonance chamber just above the glottis (the piriform recess),[8] which eliminates

8 The piriform recess is a groove in the lining of the pharynx between the hyoid bone and the thyroid cartilage. The stylopharyngeal muscle is capable of expanding the space considerably (Flach and Schwickardi, 1966).

overtones of frequencies above 5000 cycles per second. The voice thus avoids the sharp timbre for which these frequencies are responsible (Fant, 1960).

A long-standing subject of contention is whether the larynx moves up or down when the pitch of the sung note rises. A probable reason for this lack of agreement is that the position of the larynx has been assessed from the front. This may prove deceptive: measurements on the same singer may produce contrary results, as the distance between larynx and chin can suggest that the larynx is rising, while the distance between the larynx and sternum might show that it is sinking. It would be more correct to assess the position of the larynx in relation to the cervical column, and X-rays of this have shown that in fact the larynx rises with rising pitch (Sonninen, 1956, p. 83). The front of the throat is compressed in its entirety, and the distance between chin and sternum is shortened (see fig. 17).

Coverage and transitions   Parts of the 'yawn muscle' (upper pharyngeal constrictor; fig. 27, p. 49) originate on the jaw and the back of the tongue. These are movable structures and have to give way spontaneously during a yawn. The constrictor will then be tensed along a line towards the back of the pharyngeal wall. A chain reaction is initiated: breathing muscles, trachea, lowering of the larynx. (See also fig. 19, p. 32.)

The following description of the transitions is based on a relatively light type of voice, a soprano or mezzo-soprano. The corresponding transitional notes for tenors and baritones are one octave lower. The 'dark' voices, alto and bass, *may* have their transitions a semitone to a whole tone lower. One or several transitions may be 'innate'; in other words, no difficulty will be experienced in passing from one register to another.

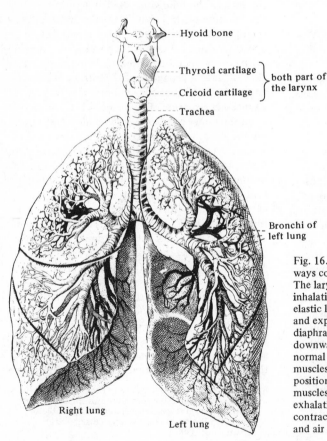

Hyoid bone

Thyroid cartilage $\Big\}$ both part of
Cricoid cartilage $\Big\}$ the larynx

Trachea

Bronchi of left lung

Right lung

Left lung

Fig. 16. The airways to the lungs, and the lungs. The airways consist of the trachea (windpipe) and the bronchi. The larynx is situated at the top of the trachea. During inhalation, when the thoracic cavity is expanded, the elastic lungs follow passively, the bronchi are stretched, and expand at the same time, so that air rushes in. The diaphragm is lowered, and the trachea is subjected to a downward pull. However, this does not mean that in normal breathing the larynx is also lowered, as the muscles above the larynx are tensed so as to hold it in position (Andrew, 1955). In a yawn, though, these muscles yield, and the larynx *is* lowered. In ordinary exhalation, the breathing muscles are relaxed, the lungs contract elastically, raising the diaphragm with them, and air rushes out. (After Benninghoff-Goerttler, 1967.)

The low register

The low register extends from b natural to b′ flat.

Exercise 30. Ascending major scale b–b′

Sing an ascending major scale starting with b natural. Repeat the scale and make sure that every note is prepared with a yawn/stretch *before* it is made to sound as the result of an expansion of the back. Feel the point of attack moving down the vertebral column as the pitch rises.

Did you have problems with the topmost interval? This interval is called the 'minor transition', and its correct performance requires additional activity.

Exercise 31. The 'minor transition' b′ flat–b′

Sing the 'minor transition' from b′ flat to b′ natural. Note that changes occur *simultaneously* in the thorax, the larynx and in the covering of the tone. In the thorax the lower serratus posterior muscle is consciously activated. Feel an expansion

of the back at the waist. Note the increased yawn/stretch from b′ flat to b′ natural.

A complicated interplay of muscles occurs in the transition to the middle register. The mouth will be *seen* to be opened wider, due to the yawn pulling at the vertical part of the lower jaw. The back of the larynx will slide up a little and move away from the cervical column, while the front is lowered and begins at the same time to incline forwards. The vocal folds are stretched passively. Covering of the tone takes place (see point (*c*) p. 28, and p. 31).

The middle register

The middle register extends from b′ natural to e″ flat.

Exercise 32. The middle register, ascending pitches

Sing the start of a major scale upwards from b′ natural. Note that the point of attack does not

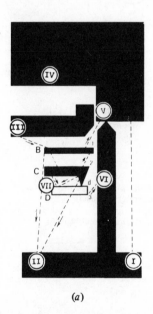

(*a*)

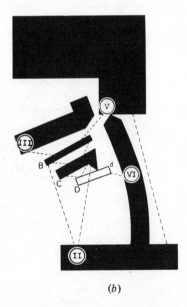

(*b*)

Fig. 17. Diagram of the larynx (see also fig. 20). A low note is sung (*a*) and then a high one (*b*). The jaw is more open for the high note than the low note. Each of the laryngeal cartilages has tipped forwards and downwards, with the chin at its furthest forward: the whole larynx has in fact 'tipped forwards'. The chain consisting of the jaw, the laryngeal cartilages and the sternum has bent the cervical column, which is shortened, and the head moves forwards on a horizontal plane. I, cervical column, dorsal side; II, sternohyoid and sternothyroid muscle; III, lower jaw; IV, head; V, stylohyoid muscle; VI, cervical column; VII, cricothyroid muscle; B, hyoid bone; C, thyroid cartilage; D, cricoid cartilage. (After Sonninen, 1956.)

move down the vertebral column, but that the muscles of the back that are involved in singing are progressively activated with increasing pitch. The pitch continues to rise as the yawn becomes stronger and the air pressure increases. The sterno-thyroid muscle (fig. 18a) extracts the last ounce out of the tensile potential of the vocal folds by drawing the thyroid cartilage forward in its joint with the cricoid cartilage, where a reasonable amount of movement is possible (Sonninen, 1956, p. 25).

Is there room for e″ natural in the upper pharynx? Repeat the exercise and note whether something happens at the interval d″ sharp to e″ natural. What happens is that the transition to head register takes place.

The transition to head register

The transition to the head register takes place at the interval e″ flat to e″ natural.

Correct performance of this transition requires the following adjustments.

(*a*) *The thorax.* The anterior serratus muscle (fig. 9) is consciously activated, *in addition to* the lower serratus posterior muscle, which is already activated.

(*b*) *The larynx.* The front of the larynx is lowered on account of the increasing yawn. The position of the larynx is drastically changed (fig. 17) because the external muscles at the front are

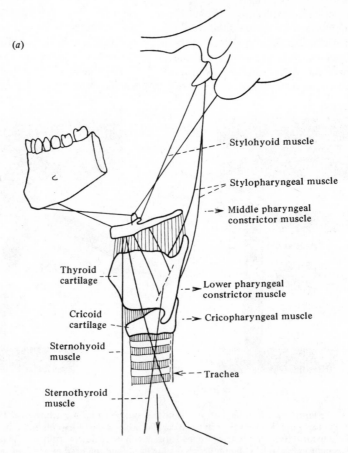

(*a*)

Fig. 18(*a*). The external muscles of the larynx. With the aid of these the larynx can be moved up/down, forwards/backwards, and it can be made to assume a more or less inclined position. Every change in the position of the larynx causes the inner structures shown in fig. 29 to react. (After Sokolowsky, 1943.)

drawing the thyroid cartilage forward, while the cricoid cartilage remains relatively stationary. The distance between the cervical column and the larynx increases significantly on account of the collective pull of the chain of muscles from the lower jaw via the larynx to the sternum. In dramatic bursts of high notes by great singers, the cranial part of the cervical column is bent forwards, while the cranium is moved forwards in the horizontal plane (fig. 17) and the neck becomes shorter and thicker (see fig. 20).

(c) *Covering the tone.* The opening of the jaw increases spontaneously, and the dorsum of the tongue is pulled back (see fig. 19). The vocal folds are lengthened, and become thinner (see pp. 49, 50). The front vowels [i] and [ε] will have a rather sharp timbre if the tone is not covered. As far as the back vowels are concerned, concentrate on articulating them with a narrow pharyngeal cavity. In addition to the covering movement, the muscles

responsible for the pulling back of the tongue (fig. 15, 2 and 3: the hyoglossus and the styloglossus muscles) produce a feeling that 'the vowel is swallowing itself'. If the transition has been correctly carried out, the tone is supported and can be run higher up with full-bodied resonance.

All the way up from the low register, the larynx has moved forwards almost imperceptibly as the pitch has risen. This can be noticed in the back vowels, particularly [ɑ], the characteristic resonance of which depends wholly on the space between the root of the tongue and the pharyngeal wall being narrow (Fant, 1960). In a rising sequence of notes the resonance must be adjusted, and the root of the tongue must follow the muscle that is exerting a backwards pull. The same applies to the back vowels [ɔ] and [ʊ], but to a lesser extent.

In some singers the dark vowels will reach a critical point between f′ sharp and b′ flat. For

(b)

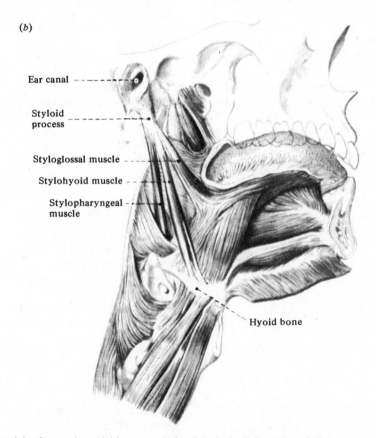

Ear canal

Styloid process

Styloglossal muscle

Stylohyoid muscle

Stylopharyngeal muscle

Hyoid bone

Fig. 18(*b*). Muscles originating on the styloid process. (After Benninghoff-Goerttler, 1967.)

31

these notes and onward a slip of lingual muscle (the chondroglossus) should be activated; this originates in front of the hyoglossus muscle, on the lesser horn of the hyoid bone (fig. 28, p. 50).

The head register

The head register extends from e″ natural upwards. Rising pitch demands ever more muscular effort. However, it must be remembered that without an increasing yawn/stretch the necessary expansion of the back and sides is impossible. Where the yawn is insufficient the larynx will suddenly move upwards to beyond the fourth cervical vertebra. The voice then 'breaks' and collapsed falsetto is the result (see below).

Head register versus falsetto

Complete confusion appears to reign among researchers and teachers of singing as to the definition of and distinction between head notes and falsetto. We believe that in the case of a head note, a proportion of the muscles of the vocal folds participate actively in the vibrations of the glottis (Rubin, Le Cover and Vennard, 1967).

The falsetto register is situated above a singer's actual vocal register (Rubin and Hirt, 1960). In collapsed falsetto the tone is supported above the navel, it has lost its volume and lower resonance, and achieves only a meagre timbre. Luchsinger (1950, p. 62) states 'the tone is poor in partials and can hardly be modulated'. Collapsed falsetto is not considered a genuine entity in singing.

An exception should be made in the case of *good* counter-tenors. These obviously make use of

a supported falsetto (Husler and Rodd-Marling, 1956), which can be modulated. The falsetto register in counter-tenors also comprises large portions of the singer's true head register. One of the present authors (H.M.B.) has a baritone voice, but sings counter-tenor in a male quartet, using a supported and easily modulated falsetto, which is clearly different from his head register. When singing supported falsetto his larynx does *not* rise above the critical fourth cervical vertebra, and the tone is supported below the navel.

Changing pitch: descending pitch

The ventral side of the cervical column: a brief guide

As stated earlier there are muscles on both the dorsal (back) and the ventral (front) sides of the vertebral column. In the various methods of singing they affect the manner of breathing, the posture, the song-stretch, and the yawn. The ventral muscles of the vertebral column consist of two systems: one in front of the cervical column, the other inside the abdominal cavity, originating on the lumbar vertebrae.

With straight fingers, palms facing forwards, and elbows jutting out sideways, push your fingers in from the sides, below the lower jaw, between the throat and the ventral side of the cervical column. This is where the ventral muscles are to be found (fig. 21).

Technique for singing a descending sequence

Remember that when singing an *ascending* sequence of notes one should concentrate on the increasing yawn/stretch (which produces tension in the diaphragm and activation of an increasing number of 'segments' of the thorax). The thorax becomes progressively broader and flatter (more ellipsoid), leading, provided the support counteracts the lowering of the diaphragm, to increased air pressure in the lungs. Where there is a lack of adequate support the breathing reflex from the yawn leads to the lowering of the diaphragm, resulting in inhalation. However, when singing a *descending* sequence of notes the thorax naturally becomes progressively *less* flattened (more circular), thus increasing its volume. If this is not

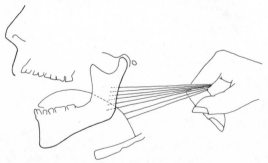

Fig. 19. Covering the tone. The attachment of the upper pharyngeal constrictor to the movable structures, i.e. the dorsum of the tongue and the jaw. In the figure the hand exerts the pull of the yawn muscle.

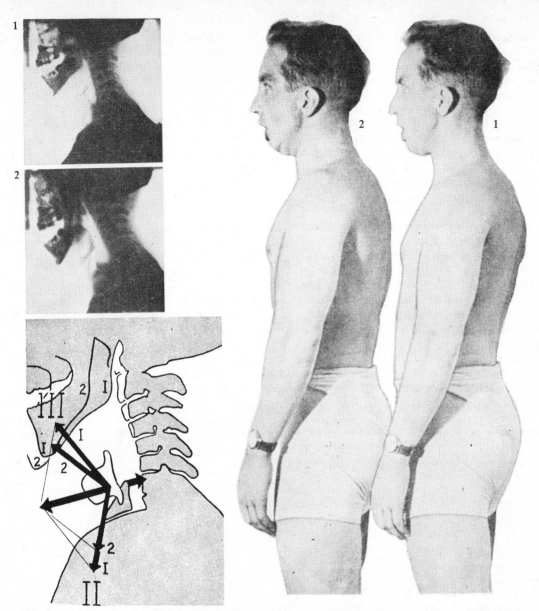

Fig. 20. Singer using the dorsal method singing a low note, G sharp (1), and a high note, a′ sharp (2). For the high note the singer's back and sides are expanded. The diagram on the left has been drawn on the basis of the X-ray photographs above. Relative to its position for the low note (1), the larynx has been drawn forwards, in 2, and the distance between chin and sternum shortened. The upper part of the cervical column is bent, and the neck is shorter and thicker. This must not be confused with the situation where the cervical column is straightened out and moves back more directly under the head, as in exercise 11 (p. 12), whilst humming a fifth. (After Sonninen, 1956.)

In 1958, at the Wenner-Gren's Institute in Stockholm, Sine Butenschøn had investigations carried out on the singer pictured above in order to discover whether or not the dorsal method resulted in the thorax changing its shape for the various vowels. Rapid X-ray photography was used, with six exposures per second. The vowels [ɔ i ɔ i ɔ i] were sung alternately at the same pitch. The result was that 'the bowels of the singer made a movement which cannot have been due to peristalsis' (Dr P.O. Gribbe, personal communication); this was taken to reflect that the bowel movements were due to the alterations of thorax shape that took place during the alternation of vowels. In 1965 Dr Arne Lundervold of the neurological department of the Rikshospitalet (National Hospital, Oslo) carried out an electromyographic investigation of the levator muscles of the ribs of Sine Butenschøn during the same vowel-singing exercise described above. The result was that these muscles were activated more for [i] than for [ɔ] (A. Lundervold, personal communication).

33

compensated for, the pressure in the lungs will be lost and cause the tone to fade. The support must therefore be correspondingly increased, pressing the diaphragm into the thorax to maintain the necessary pressure in the lungs.

As an example, we can take the minor transition from b′ to b′ flat, i.e. from the middle register to the low register. At b′ flat the lower serratus posterior muscle is shifted, and the need for support increases spontaneously. In exercise 11 (p. 12), humming the interval of a fifth, the deeper note was achieved by yawning 'further in and higher up'. The result was that the cervical column was thus stretched as its ventral muscles were activated, straightening out the normal curvature of the cervical vertebrae. With the increasing need for support in a descending sequence of notes, as more and more 'segments' of the thorax cease to be involved in the singing process (in the reverse order to which they are brought into play in an ascending sequence), the activity of the ventral muscles of the cervical column will be more and more assisted by the corresponding activity of the iliopsoas muscle (fig. 22). Rather suddenly the iliopsoas becomes the dominant muscle system. This sudden change takes place at a pitch 'area' known as *das Loch der Frauenstimme*, literally 'the hole in a woman's voice'. If sufficient support is not forthcoming here, the singer will suddenly be left without breath. The crisis may occur on f′ as well as on d′ or c′. If, however, one allows the iliopsoas to take the lead in the stretch, whilst leaving the cervical muscular activity unchanged, the support will adjust to the note. The result will be no *Loch* and no difficulty in breath control. (The name 'hole in a *woman's* voice' may be explained by the characteristic shape of the female pelvis (deeper and broader than that of the male) and the compensatory greater curvature in the lumbar vertebrae, which influences the direction of force and thus the action of the iliopsoas in women.)

Exercise 33

Sing a descending sequence of notes, starting with a′. Do you experience any particular difficulty? Are you caught without breath at e′ or d′? Then, sing slowly a chromatic descending sequence of notes starting with a′. Notice whether or not the tone falls on f′, d′ or c′. Feel what happens in your support area, and try to compensate for the

failure by increasing the support: yawn higher up and further back, so that the iliopsoas as well as the support area will be increasingly engaged, controlling your tone.

Exercise 34

Sing over and over again your critical intervals e.g.

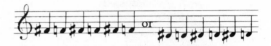

Listen to both the pitches, not only to the deeper one. Prepare each note before singing it by making the appropriate adjustments of yawn/stretch. Feel the effect on the support area.

Exercise 35

Sing *legato* over and over again, initially with a back vowel ([ɑ] or [ɔ.]):

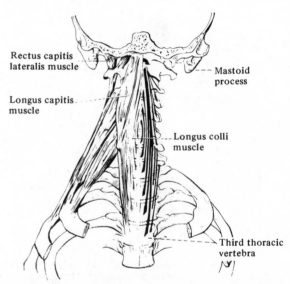

Rectus capitis lateralis muscle

Longus capitis muscle

Mastoid process

Longus colli muscle

Third thoracic vertebra

Fig. 21. The ventral muscles of the head (longus capitis) and of the neck (longus colli). These muscles extend from the base of the skull (just in front of the foramen magnum) in the form of long narrow strips along both sides of the seven cervical vertebrae, and act to shorten the cervical column in front, straightening out its otherwise normal curvature. They also continue along the three uppermost thoracic vertebrae. When unstressed vowels are sung, this portion of the musculature expands the thorax. When singing staccato, it 'snatches the tone'. (After Benninghoff-Goerttler, 1968).

Sing the ascending notes, feeling that the song-stretch increases, involving more and more thoracic 'segments'.

At the moment of 'reversing direction', at the very beginning of the descent, the yawn/stretch preparation of the first note down (g') will be decisive for the performance of the whole descending sequence of notes. On the top note (a') prepare the g' by yawning 'along the correct path', which is felt to be 'behind and up'.

On reaching the bottom note (d'), prepare e' with the yawn/stretch *before* the note is sung.

Exercise 36

Sing *legato* a descending fifth, beginning with a'. Prepare the lower note by yawning it 'up behind' while the first note is still being sung, then release the lower note by attacking higher up in the back. Feel the support.

Exercise 37

(1) Sing *legato* a sequence of alternately ascending and descending fifths, beginning on d'. Make sure that the tongue and the jaw 'give way' in advance of the upper note, as a result of the increased yawn.

(2) Add the interval of a third to the above

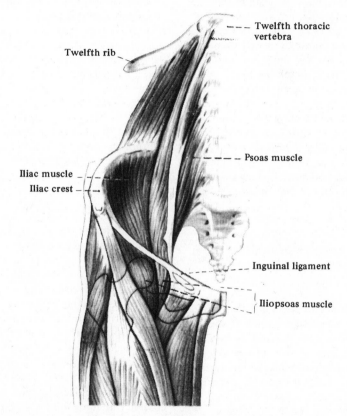

Fig. 22. The iliopsoas muscle. This is activated together with the ventral muscles of the cervical column. The degree of yawn/stretch will control the relative tension between them.

The iliopsoas consists of two parts: the lumbar portion or psoas muscle, which originates on the ventral side of the lumbar vertebrae, and the iliac muscle, which originates in the concavity of the hip bone (ilium). The two parts join a common tendon which attaches them to the inside of the thigh bone (femur).

The iliopsoas is enveloped in a sheet of fibrous tissue which in the groin joins with the inguinal (groin) ligament. Since the lower parts of the three broad muscles of the abdomen also originate on the inguinal ligament, a mutual inter-effect is created in the 'support area' (fig. 6) between the iliopsoas and the abdominal muscles. (After Benninghoff-Goerttler, 1968.)

exercise, singing a sequence of ascending and descending major triads.

Move both (1) and (2) chromatically up and down.

Exercise 38. Pitching the tone in the head register

Sing e″, using handhold no. 3 (p. 19) whenever a vowel with protruded lips is involved. Don't take a breath! Yawn/stretch sufficiently to enable you to feel the preparation of the note at the sides of the rib-cage, due to the action of the serratus anterior muscle. This you can do *without* having 'taken' a breath. If you cannot reach as high as e″ in this way, your yawn/stretch has been too weak.

When singing e″, feel the effort both in the lumbar region and under your arms: the entire dorsal portion of the thorax is expanded. Imitate the action of a pressure pump; the vowel sound is at the *bottom* of the body and the pump handle in the yawned vowel shape. Fetch the sound up, vomit it out! If you don't succeed, remember the three transformations necessary in (*a*) the thorax, (*b*) the larynx and (*c*) the covering of the tone (pp. 30–2). Check to see that they are there. Don't sing a small and rather anxious attacking tone, which will teach you nothing. Howl, scream the note, sing badly: if you do, following these guidelines, the result won't in fact be bad!

Transition to the middle register

The transition to the middle register takes place at the interval e″ to d″ sharp.

Exercise 39

Sing e″ according to exercise 38 and then continue *legato* with a descending sequence of notes. While you are still on e″, yawn/stretch 'up behind' to pitch the d″. If you don't yawn sufficiently, the tone will 'jump into your mouth'. Prepare and execute each note. The further down the note is in the sequence, the more the song-stretch in the cervical regions will involve the lumbar region.

Transition to the low register

The transition to the low register takes place at the interval b′ to b′ flat. On reaching this interval the lower serratus posterior muscle is no longer active.

Exercise 40

(1) Sing *legato* a descending sequence of notes, starting with b′. You are faced with the same problems as in exercise 39, but to a greater extent. Again the second note (a′) must be sufficiently prepared by the yawn/stretch before you leave the first note (b′).

(2) Repeat the procedure of exercise 36, but this time using a descending octave starting on b′.

Transition to the very low register

The transition to the very low register takes place at the interval b to b flat.

Exercise 41

Sing the interval b natural to b flat; listen to the tone. If b flat is weak and air escapes through the glottis, you have yawned insufficiently. From b flat downwards, the maintenance of sufficient air pressure is dependent on two muscles in the front of the thorax: the transverse muscle (fig. 23) and the pectoralis minor muscle (fig. 9, p. 15). When the ribs are held in a fixed position the transverse muscle of the thorax draws the sternum in, so that the thoracic cavity is flattened. At the same time the pectoralis minor muscle makes the thorax broader.

Transition to the deepest register

The transition to the deepest register occurs at the interval f sharp to f natural.

Exercise 42

Sing the interval f sharp to f natural. If you succeed, feel the big change that occurs inside your throat when the lower note is pitched. To arrive at f natural from f sharp demands a change of the angle between the head and the larynx (fig. 24). Correctly performed, that is with extreme yawning 'up and *behind*', the back of the head is actively *lifted* in its joint with the vertebral column ('nodding joint'), by contraction of the ventral muscles in the cervical region (fig. 21). The result is perceived as a releasing, an opening of a trapdoor in the pharynx that expands the room for tone resonance.

Mistake. If you simply pull your chin in and down you 'press' the tone down, you 'sit on the note', the note 'falls down on the glottis', resulting in a strained sound. In the bass section of inferior choirs, chins are regularly seen to disappear into collars on low pitches.

Monnier (1970) claims that the deepest possible note for a contralto is F. For a bass it is an octave lower, i.e. F, which is 43.2 cycles per second.

Simultaneous change of pitch and vowel

Changes of pitch and vowel do not occur at absolutely the same time. Whilst pitch no. 1 is sung, e.g. on [ɔ], pitch no. 2 is yawn/stretched. The quantity of sound is reduced. Next, the vowel form of, for example, [ɩ] is re-yawned. Pitch no. 1 will still sound. As the air pressure in the lungs is changed, pitch no. 2 will sound on the second vowel. Remember that the tone is released in the vertebral column, except in the very deep register, when the pressure is released by the transverse muscles of the thorax (fig. 23) and the oblique cervical muscle (fig. 24).

Exercise 43. Changing both pitch and vowel
Repeat exercise 26, where the vowel changes on the same pitch. Then carry out exercises 34 to 37 singing bright and dark vowels on alternate notes. Transpose the exercises chromatically through all the registers.

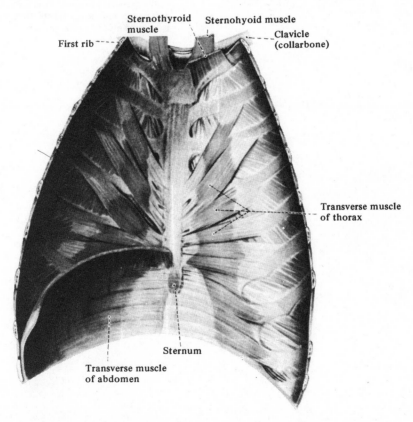

Fig. 23. The transverse muscle on the inner surface of the thorax, seen from behind. The muscle connects the sternum with ribs two to six. (After W. Heidegger (1961). *Atlas der Anatomie*, vol. 1.)

37

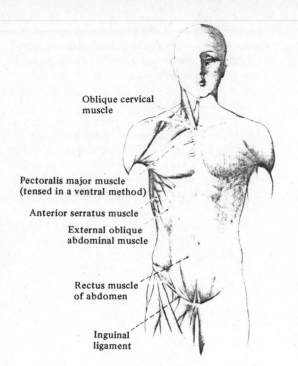

Oblique cervical
muscle

Pectoralis major muscle
(tensed in a ventral method)

Anterior serratus muscle

External oblique
abdominal muscle

Rectus muscle
of abdomen

Inguinal
ligament

Fig. 24. The oblique cervical muscle. This muscle originates partly on the clavicle (collarbone), and partly on the
sternum, then slants upwards and backwards and attaches
to the mastoid process behind the ear. The direction of
pull of this muscle on the sternum is upwards, while the
transverse muscle of the thorax pulls the sternum in.

7

Consonants

All consonants contain an element of noise (Fant, 1960). They may consist entirely of noise: e.g. *f*, *p*, *t*, unvoiced *th* [θ], *k*, and the sibilants *s*, *sh* [ʃ] and *ch* [tʃ]. Alternatively they may be voiced (i.e. having an element of voice): e.g. *l*, *m*, *n*, voiced *th* [ð], *ng*, *v*, voiced *r*, and the voiced sibilants [dʒ] as in *judge*, *z* as in *buzz* and [ʒ] as in pleasure. *L* is the only consonant that 'leaks out' into the cheeks. If *s* is pronounced in the same way, the result is a speech defect.

Articulators

Articulators for consonants are the tongue, lips and lower jaw. *H* is the only consonant which originates only in the glottis. Unlike the vowels, which require a closing of the glottis, *h* requires a half-open glottis (Fant, 1960).

The tongue

The tip of the tongue provides an obstruction for *t*, *d*, *th*, *n*, *l*. For the sibilant *sh* [ʃ], as in *shirt*, the tip is slightly lowered and withdrawn and the air escapes between the tongue and the upper jaw. The tip of the tongue vibrates for lingual *r*, and the blade of the tongue is raised against the palate for *y* (*yes*). The dorsum of the tongue provides an obstruction for *k*, *g*, and *ng*. The uvular *r* is not used in classical art singing.

The lips

The labial consonants, i.e. those formed by the lips, are *p*, *b* and *m*, while the labial-dental consonants *f* and *v* are formed by the upper teeth against the lower lip. In Germanic languages *p*, *t* and *k* are pronounced with an open glottis, and are followed by an *h* sound, i.e. they are aspirated. These consonants are pronounced in the Romance languages (and in Finnish) with a closed glottis (Selmer and Broch, 1950). They produce a slight explosive sound. *B*, *d* and *g* are likewise aspirated in the Germanic languages but not in the Romance languages.

The lower jaw

The lower jaw takes part in the pronunciation of the labial consonants *m*, *b* and *p*, the labial-dental consonants *f* and *v*, and the sibilant consonants *sh* [ʃ] and *ch* [tʃ]. *S* demands an almost closed jaw in order to prevent lisping.

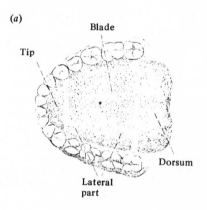

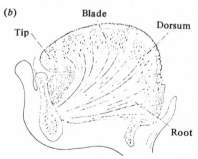

Fig. 25. The tongue seen (*a*) from above (*b*) from the side.

Tongue, lips and jaw are the articulators common to consonants and vowels, but the upper pharynx and the vocal shape of the thorax serve the vowel alone (see chapter 5). Behind each sung consonant there must at all times be a yawned, breath-controlling vowel, irrespective of whether the consonant comes before or after the vowel. In other words, one moves from vowel to vowel and the consonants, singly or in groups, 'come in between'.

The vocal colouring of the consonant

Protruded lips, which characterise a dark vowel, also give the consonant a dark colouring, as, for example, the *s* in o*s*so. Vowels with passive lips, on the other hand, give consonants a bright colouring, e.g. i*s*si. The tongue position for the vowel, too, plays a role. Consonants with front vowels, such as [˙] and [ɛ], are brighter than those combined with the back vowel [ɑ].

When the syllable starts with a consonant, it warns the listener of the following vowel and, immediately and unconsciously, brings the 'guessing mechanism' into operation (Stevens and House, 1972).

Exercise 44. The consonant *l*
Behind the voiced consonant *l* the vowel can be both maintained and changed.

Place the tip of the tongue against the corrugated edge of the palate (i.e. the area between the sockets holding the roots of the top teeth and the palatal vault). The *l* is articulated during this exercise a little further back in the oral cavity than in normal speech. Let the tip of the tongue *remain in position* while the sequence of vowels [ɪ] [ɑ] [ɔ] [u] is sung *legato* on the same pitch. Check that the tongue remains in position!

Exercise 45. l articulated between vowels
Sing the same vowels as in exercise 44 above, but this time ensure that the tip of the tongue carries out a movement and articulates *l*. The vowel timbre should be unaffected by the consonant: [ɪ l ɪ l ɪ l ɪ l ɪ], [ɑ l ɑ l ɑ l ɑ l ɑ], [u l u l u l u l u]. Listen and note that the *l* in the [ɪ l ɪ] group is clear and bright, and in the [u l u] group dark. This can be heard still more distinctly

when bright and dark vowels are grouped around *l*: e.g. [ɪ l ɑ], [ɛ l u]. That is to say, sing [ɪ], yawn [ɑ], sing [l ɑ]; sing [ɛ], yawn [u], sing [l u] ; conversely, sing [u], yawn [ɪ], sing [l ɪ], and so on. With the yawned vowel behind it, the consonant can be articulated clearly. If the consonant demands the use of the jaw in its articulation, and especially if the vowel is to be pronounced with protruding lips, consonants will tend to affect the proper vowel timbre. Each vowel is created by a characteristic pattern of shapes involving the pharynx, tongue and lips, and in singing this pattern must be maintained consistently to ensure a good vowel and tone quality.

Exercise 46. Consonant between two identical vowels
Sing [ɔ f ɔ f ɔ f ɔ f ɔ]. Be careful to maintain the characteristics of the vowel throughout. Use of handhold no. 3 (p. 19) may be helpful, as this will prevent a closing movement of the jaw on *f* but will aid the maintenance of the yawn and thus of the proper vowel timbre. Do this even though the handhold makes the correct pronunciation of the consonant impossible. The same applies to *v*, *m*, *b*, *p*, *sh* and *s*.

Sing [u m u m u m u], and other vowel–consonant combinations.

Exercise 47. Consonant between two different vowels
Sing [ɔ b ɪ ɔ b ɪ ɔ b ɪ], [ɪ p u ɪ p u ɪ p u], and so on. Prepare with the appropriate yawn/ stretch on the preceding vowel *before* the consonant is pronounced, so that the consonant is 'drawn' into the new vowel's resonance cavity. Thus the new vowel gets its proper timbre while the consonant is coloured by the vowel. Whilst keeping the upper pharynx in the vowel shape, articulate the consonant clearly. Even when the consonant forces the lower jaw to close, the vowel timbre will not be affected. The upper laryngeal constrictor will not let go its hold on the jaw.

Colouring the consonant with the vowel gives the listener an *illusion* of hearing uninterrupted sound, even when unvoiced consonants actually break the vocalisation. (It is probably here that the secret behind the fluency of *bel canto* singing lies.)

40

Exercise 48

With exercise 47 in mind, sing the following example from Handel's *Messiah*, where three

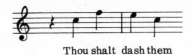

Thou shalt dash them

adjacent consonants occur in the sentence 'Thou shalt dash them'. The [a] vowel in *shalt* and *dash*

is maintained whilst *lt* in *shalt* and *d* in *dash* are sung, coloured by [a]. Then [a] in *dash* is changed to [ε], and then is sung with *them* coloured by [ε].

Mistake. Let us suppose that the syllable has a dark vowel necessitating protruded lips, and that the preceding consonant is sung without protruding lips. The listener still expects to hear an [ε] or [e] or [a], but instead a dark vowel is sung. This is confusing, and the *th* of *them* is coloured by [ε].

8

Other aspects of tone production

Volume versus pitch

If the position of the larynx and glottis remains unchanged, volume will increase and pitch will rise as air pressure increases in the lungs. In this case the increased air pressure will cause the note literally to slide upwards (*glissando*). However, it is possible to control both the air pressure and the tension/thickness/length of the vocal folds, so by listening critically to the note the necessary adjustments can be made to maintain the same pitch even when the volume is changed, or vice versa.

Exercise 49. Raising the pitch whilst maintaining a constant volume

Sing *glissando* up and down on [ɔ] (and then on other vowels). Repeat the exercise, trying to keep the volume constant, and maintaining the proper vowel timbre by adjusting the yawn, and the song-stretch in the back. Make sure that the dorsum of the tongue as well as the lower jaw slides back/open with the increasing yawn. This is crucial for maintaining the vowel sound.

Exercise 50. Increasing volume (crescendo) on the same pitch

Sing a note. *Crescendo* and *decrescendo* on it over and over again. Feel that when you make a *crescendo* the intercostal muscles of the ribs within the stretched area have the intensity of their activity *consciously* increased towards greater strength, and that, provided a yawn further lowers the larynx, the back expands.

On *fortissimo* and *pianissimo*

Singing in the head register, not only in *forte* but also in *piano* passages, must involve a head-tone quality. The larynx must be lower than the fourth cervical vertebra (see p. 32); it should, in fact, be as low as possible for any given pitch, otherwise the result will be *falsetto*. Both lower serratus posterior and serratus anterior muscles must expand the back. In all registers the upper pharynx should preserve the vowel shape. In soft singing the tone should be covered to the same degree as in loud singing, but the expanding muscles of the back will only be *slightly* activated for soft singing. It will take some time before the right balance between the various forces involved is discovered. For instance, you should sing only *forte* or *mezzo-forte* in the head register until you are sure *not* to switch over to *falsetto* when the volume falls below these levels. *Pianissimo* with full resonance in the head register is a feature of great singing.

On shouting versus singing

In shouting there is always an element of forced laryngeal sound or noise. The support is transformed into abdominal pressure (fig. 6, p. 13), the ribs squeeze the lungs, and the thorax is not flattened but constricted. In singing it is permissible to use the shouting tone as an expression of power, might or brutality, but it is damaging to the voice, and its frequent use will lead to a progressive shortening of the upper register.

The performance of stressed and unstressed vowels

The stressed vowel is sung with a conscious expansion of the back, which allows the volume of the note to increase towards a peak, decreasing afterwards to its initial volume. The back is expanded as the yawn is increased and the larynx thereby lowered. For this purpose the tone must be covered by means of the yawn/stretch.

The path of the unstressed vowel is situated behind that of the stressed, and is yawned higher up in the pharynx. The ventral muscles of the cervical column extending down to the upper three thoracic vertebrae are used (fig. 21). The back expands at the topmost ribs and the unstressed vowel then sounds. Unstressed vowels have a constant volume.

NB: The relationship between stressed/ unstressed vowels is not the same as that between strong/weak, articulatorily distinct/blurred, or resonantly clear/diffuse.

Exercise 51. Stressed and unstressed notes on the same vowel
On the same vowel, sing

Stress the dotted notes. Then vary the vowels, placing bright and dark vowels alternately, one note to each. Alternate stressed vowels with an unstressed, yawned [ə].

On rhythm and time (metre)

Rhythm in singing is an alternation of stressed and unstressed syllables, generally according to a definite pattern. In the dorsal method the singer experiences rhythm as something physical. As described under the section on stressed and unstressed vowels above, rhythm is marked by alternate singing of stressed vowels (with expansion in the back) and unstressed vowels (with expansion in the upper part of the back of the thorax). All vowels must actually *sound* in the same resonance cavity.

Time may be defined as a framework or system of intonation to which the rhythmic patterns are subordinate: e.g. different parts of a waltz may have varying rhythmic patterns, but they are all within waltz time.

Stressing the diphthong

The following phonetic symbols will be used to indicate the English diphthongs:

[ɑ ɪ]	as in *my*
[ɔ ɪ]	as in *boy*
[e ɪ]	as in *play*
[ɛ ə]	as in *hair*
[ɪ ə]	as in *dear*
[j u ə]	as in *pure*
[o u]	as in *no*
[a u]	as in *how*

The diphthong consists of two vowels within the same syllable. In the Germanic languages the first element is stressed in relation to the second. In rapid speech the unstressed, second element often disappears. In singing the unstressed vowel must be yawned far back and right up in the resonance cavity, among other things to ensure proper control of breathing.

The syllable must be sung on the first vowel and the second vowel 'snatched up' behind it, at the last moment.

Exercise 52. Stressing the diphthong
Sing the following extract from Handel's *Messiah*

But who may a - bide the day

which has the diphthongs [e ɪ] (in *may*), [ɑ ɪ] (in *abide*) and [e ɪ] (in *day*). Make sure that the *un*stressed vowels are also properly executed, otherwise you will lose breath. If there are several notes to a syllable they are all sung on the first vowel sound. Re-yawning for the second, unstressed vowel occurs, as already mentioned, *at the very last moment* before the next syllable is tackled.

Exercise 53. Changing note on one diphthong

but who may a - bide

Don't forget to articulate the second, unstressed part of the diphthong. Unstressed vowels are characteristic of languages with strong stresses (Lindblom, 1963). In the Romance languages the diphthong is far more developed in speech; the

43

second element is emphasised just as often as the first, and the two do not weaken one another. Thus in Italian we have *piano*, *piego*, *fiore*, *uomo*, *chiudo*, etc. The pronunciation of the diphthongs is not the least of the reasons why Italian is so suitable a language for singing.

Stressing a syllable

When a syllable is stressed, the vowel can either be attacked *piano* and undergo a *crescendo/decrescendo* as explained on p. 42, or it can be attacked and maintained at full strength.

Exercise 54. The stressed syllable attacked piano
Sing the following example from Caccini's *Amarilli*:

A-ma - ri – – – lli

Attack the syllable *ri piano* and perform a controlled modest swell.

On the other hand, if the vowel is attacked and maintained at full strength, it expresses power, strong emotions, or marked rhythm. Feel how the yawn makes the pharynx give way and allows the back to expand.

Exercise 55. The stressed syllable attacked forte
Sing the extract below from Handel's *Messiah*. In this case the consonant should allow itself to be 'sucked into' the vowel, while at the same time resisting, with a force corresponding to the strength of the vowel. The consonant is forced to release its hold on the place of articulation — lip or palate — and a small plosion or catch in the transition to the vowel can be heard.

The trill

The trill is a rapid exchange between two notes, which the singer performs in alternation. In classical music the *trillo maggiore* is the main form. The interval in this case is a whole tone, but trills with the interval of a semitone are also common. The trill is primarily a matter of hearing-anticipation. The singer must imagine both notes at once. The deeper one is the main note (the melody note) and this is stressed, although it was customary before the beginning of the nineteenth century to start the trill on the upper of the two notes (the subsidiary or non-melody note), a feature which renders less serious the problem to be outlined below. In other words, the singer must concentrate on a clear precise subsidiary note, or this note is liable to disappear. Here again the tendency to sing the unstressed note imprecisely or unclearly is encountered. If the interval is sung slowly, in order to train the feedback control from the ear, there will be a feeling of singing up/down, i.e. subsidiary note/main note.

Exercise 56. Singing a trill
Adjust your yawn for the main note, while staying prepared for a *supplementary* yawn/stretch which will provide the subsidiary note. The execution of this will be felt as a forwards/backwards movement in the pharynx. This is because the yawn/stretch remains unchanged, the changing of the note taking place only in the upper pharynx. The speed of the trill appears to be a purely natural phenomenon, a heavy, dark voice having fewer pulses per second than a light, bright one. However, if the movement is four pulses per second or less, the ear is capable of distinguishing the up-and-down movement and this produces an unpleasant effect.

Grace notes

Grace notes are ornamental notes that borrow time from the value of the note to which they

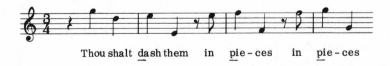

Thou shalt dash them in pie - ces in pie - ces

belong. During practice the passage should first be sung *without* the grace notes, as in example (*a*), to ensure correct metre, time and rhythm.

Exercise 57. Singing grace notes
Sing the following examples:

Grace notes and *coloratura* are technically executed like any other notes, in that the note is prepared and then sung. It may be seen as a chase, the preparation always ahead, but hotly pursued

by the note. Accuracy in singing grace notes and *coloratura* is in fact a question of anticipation and 'hearing' both notes together, while *aiming* at each individual note.

The pause

There are two kinds of pause, both of which are illustrated by the following extract from *Amarilli*. This example has three melodic phrases. The full-stop pause comes after phrase I has been sung, the comma pause before phrase III.

Exercise 58. The full-stop pause
Sing the example above. At the first pause the yawn/stretch is released, and phrase II is then prepared by means of a new yawn/stretch.

Phrase II is on the way to the climax which is reached in phrase III, and not until this is reached does the melody line reach its peak and the *crescendo* its full strength. Between the two phrases is a comma pause.

Exercise 59. The comma pause
Sing from phrase II. At the pause song-stretch and vocal yawn part company. On the last vowel of phrase II, (Amarill)*i*, the c″ frequency is stretched to c″ sharp, and *the stretch is maintained throughout the pause*, but with the glottis open. Air flows in on the comma pause, unobserved by singer or listener. This happens just as the vowel is being re-yawned for the stressed *A*(marilli) in phrase III, stressed because of the emotional outburst culminating in *fortissimo* Amarīlli.

How to practise a song

First, re-read the following: p. 37, simultaneous change of pitch and vowel; exercise 47, articulation of a consonant between two vowels; p. 43 on rhythm and time.

Each of the three phrases of the extract from *Amarilli* above should be worked through in the following way:

(1) Phrase I should be vocalised (i.e. without consonants). You will acquire an ear for the exaggerated articulation and for the carriage of the melody when singing *legato*. This is done by preparing the next pitch and then singing the note and vowel. The rhythm is defined by stressed/unstressed vowels.

(2) Repeat the above but this time *think* in terms of consonants, and note whether or not in so doing the vowels revert to their spoken, incomplete form.

(3) Sing the phrase with the full text. The form of the yawned vowel should be maintained 'behind' the consonants. Although these are pronounced very clearly, they will not affect the vowel configuration of the back of the pharynx. The song should be treated as a series of vowels, with the consonants coming in between.

Phrase II is then practised in the same way, followed by phrase I and phrase II consecutively, separated by the full-stop pause. This process is extended until the whole song has been so treated.

Professional singers do vocalising exercises every day. The sung vowel is always liable to decay, regressing to the spoken vowel. The vowel which is completely formed has the richest resonance and the greatest scope for varied expression.

Appendixes: Anatomy and physiology

These appendixes are included in order to familiarise the reader with the anatomical and physiological basis of the singing function; purely subjective notions should never be wholly relied on.

Appendix 1. Muscular function

The active state of a muscle is termed contraction (or sometimes 'activated', or 'tensed'). When used in this physiological sense contraction does not necessarily imply a decrease in length, but the result is of a 'pull'. When a muscle is not active it is said to be relaxed; it is not able actively to increase its length (i.e. it cannot 'push'). Movement is therefore achieved by pairs of muscles, each muscle having an antagonist whose contraction counteracts and/or nullifies the effect of the first muscle. For example, when one is gazing up at the sky, the muscles at the back of the neck are contracted and their antagonists, the throat muscles, are relaxed. If from this position one wants to look down at the ground, the throat muscles must be contracted and their antagonists, in the back of the neck, relaxed. Muscles participating in the same function are called synergists. It is the co-ordinated interplay between antagonists and synergists that makes possible a balanced and finely tuned muscular function.

Muscular contraction may be *voluntary*. Voluntary contraction can produce altered tension patterns in remote muscle groups, especially if the muscles involved have developed from the same primitive origin. For example, compensatory articulation of the broad vowels [i], [e] and [ɛ] involves contraction of the styloglossus and stylopharyngeal muscles, which pull the head slightly forwards. Regardless of the tone pitch, this triggers tension in the row of thoracic levator muscles that expand the back. The explanation of this must be sought in the prehistory of the levator muscles (J. Torgersen, personal communication).[9]

Muscular contraction can also be *reflex*, i.e. independent of the will (Brodal, 1952). For example, impulses from the upper pharynx cause the reflex contraction of the muscles involved in breathing (Nail, Sterling and Widdicombe, 1969) and impulses from the glottis a reflex contraction of the support area in the abdominal wall (Tomori, Widdicombe and Chechoslov, 1969).

Skill and efficiency in singing entail adjustment, either conscious or learned, of the degree of tension required in individual muscles, so that the effect corresponds to the intention. The aim should be to ensure that this adjustment is achieved as a reflex: for example, the singer should naturally adopt a posture that will allow the desired breathing and support reflexes to be set in motion.

Appendix 2. The constrictor muscles of the pharynx

Lower pharyngeal constrictor

The origin of the constrictor muscles in the pharynx (figs. 26 and 27) and larynx provides a key to the tensing of the glottis. According to

---

9 In reptiles the levator muscles of ribs are developed along the entire length of the vertebral column. In the higher mammals the ribs are vestigial in the cervical and lumbar regions, where they occur merely as transverse processes of the vertebrae. The same fate has been suffered by the levator muscles of these ribs, of which only vestiges remain between the transverse processes. The rectus capitis lateralis muscle of the head (fig. 21) marks the uppermost part of the system, but the whole system is of the same fundamental type (J. Torgersen, personal communication). When the broad vowels are articulated and the head moves forwards, the rectus capitis lateralis is tensed and acts as a trigger to the tensing of the entire row of levator muscles, irrespective of whether the tone is high or low.

Minnigerode (1967) these muscles were developed from a homogeneous system of constrictors. During the course of evolution a special constrictor developed out of this system, forming the *interior* constrictor system of the larynx, viz. the interior laryngeal muscles (see fig. 32, p. 52). At the mammal stage the thyroid cartilage of the larynx originated, which divided the *external* constrictor system into a dorsal (back) and ventral (front) part. At the back of the larynx the lower pharyngeal constrictor arose, and at the front the 'vocal fold tensor', the cricothyroid muscle. The outer and inner muscle systems of the larynx have, in other words, a common origin, and as the system of nervous control of muscles is seldom altered during the development of species (Barnicol, 1953) they will largely be controlled by the same parts of the central nervous system. For their function, see appendix 3.

Middle pharyngeal constrictor

The middle pharyngeal constrictor helps to determine the position of the hyoid bone, and plays a part in the general shortening of the pharynx when swallowing (Bosma, 1957).[10]

The upper pharyngeal constrictor

The functions of the upper pharyngeal constrictor during singing are in the yawn, in covering of the tone, and in determining the shape of the pharynx. The derivatives of this muscle – the levator muscle of the soft palate, the palatopharyngeal muscle and the palatothyroideus muscle (Bosma and Fletcher, 1962) – function in shaping the vowels in the pharynx.

10 The trachea and the diaphragm are drawn up during the swallowing process. This is immediately followed by exhalation.

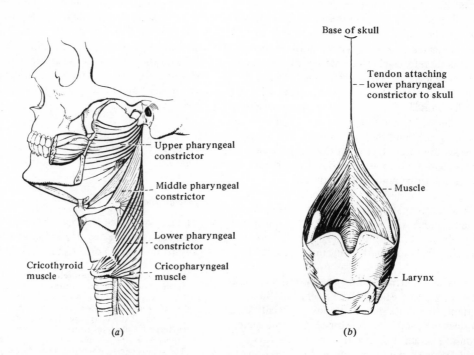

Fig. 26. (*a*) The muscles of the pharynx. (*b*) The lower pharyngeal constrictor, seen from the front, suspended from the base of the skull. The three pharyngeal constrictors are attached by a ligament to the base of the skull, from where they arch forwards and enclose the pharynx. All three slope from front to back, and only the lowermost portion of the lower pharyngeal constrictor is transverse. (According to Minnigerode (1967) parts of the transverse layer of the lower pharyngeal constrictor entangle with the sphincter muscle of the oesophagus, which is 'strangled' in the higher register.) (After Benninghoff-Goerttler, 1967.)

48

Appendix 3. The larynx

The larynx (figs. 18, 28, 29, 32) is the centre of an interplay of the following functions: (1) passive tensing of the vocal cords (vocal ligaments); (2) active tensing of the vocal folds; (3) opening and shutting of the glottis (see fig. 32). In addition the whole larynx moves up and down in relation to the cervical column (fig. 18).

During phonation the cricothyroid muscle is activated, pulling down the thyroid cartilage 'like a visor' (Kotby *et al.*, 1970) (fig. 32*d*), while the dorsal extension of the cricothyroid muscle, the lower pharyngeal constrictor, pulls the cricoid cartilage dorsally (i.e. towards the alimentary canal and the back wall of the pharynx). The result is that the vocal cords (plicae vocalis: fig. 29) are passively stretched and, at the same time, the muscles of the vocal folds are activated. The inner

muscles (fig. 32*a*, *b*, *c*) and the outer muscle (fig. 32*d*) are always activated simultaneously (Buchtal and Faaborg-Andersen, 1964); this is because they have a common origin (see appendix 2).

The position of the larynx is determined by its external muscles (fig. 18*a*) and the pharyngeal constrictor muscle. With any kind of inhalation the larynx is subjected to a downward pull by the trachea (windpipe), which is itself pulled down by the lowering of the diaphragm which causes air passage into the lungs. In ordinary inhalation, however, the muscles that raise the tongue and pharynx are tensed so as to hold the larynx in position (Andrew, 1955). In a yawn this tension disappears, the larynx is lowered, and the pharynx is extended. When the thoracic cavity is flattened (by the serratus muscles) and the abdominal wall acts as a support, this results in increased air pressure against the tensed vocal folds. Air is

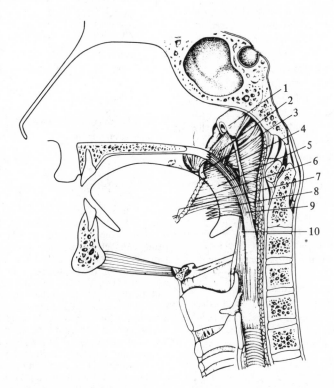

Fig. 27. The upper pharyngeal constrictor with its derivatives. The upper pharyngeal constrictor is attached by a tendon to the base of the skull (fig. 26*b*). The muscle has a complicated attachment on structures that are partly fixed and partly movable. It is attached to the side walls of the upper pharynx, the hamulus (3), a bridge of ligament to the inside of the angle of the jaw (5, 6), the actual angle of the jaw (7) and the root of the tongue (8). Its derivatives are the levator muscle of the soft palate (2), the palatopharyngeal muscle (4), which is partly supplied by a slip from the Eustachian tube (1), and the palatothyroideus muscle (10). (After Ciba *Medical Illustrations*, vol. 3, part 1.)

forced out, and the vocal folds are made to vibrate (compare p. 4).

A lowered larynx makes the voice euphonious and full-bodied

When the larynx is lowered the vocal folds become relatively relaxed and thick. In addition, the vocal tract is long, with a comparatively open ventricle (fig. 29). These factors jointly account for the full-bodied resonance that is heard. The beneficial influence of a lowered larynx on the resonance of the voice can be explained in terms of acoustics and phonetics, and the interested reader is referred to the specialist literature on the subject (e.g. Malmberg, 1968).

The vocal folds when singing low notes and high notes

During vocalisation the muscular mass of the vocal folds that takes part in the vibrations decreases as the pitch rises (fig. 30). The explanation is to be found both in the direction of pull of the connective tissue fibres that line the larynx and the trachea internally, and in the relationship of the vocal muscle to these fibres (Mayet, 1955; see fig. 31). Generally speaking, connective tissue will develop fibres running in the same direction as the constant pull to which it is exposed. In the vocal cords (vocal ligaments) the pull is horizontal, i.e. in the longitudinal direction of the vocal cord, between the angle of the thyroid cartilage in front and the vocal process of the arytenoid cartilages at the back (Mayet, 1955). This pull is situated medially, close to the glottis. In the conus elasticus, the elastic membrane of the larynx, the fibres of the connective tissue have an oblique and vertical direction of pull (fig. 31), following the downward pull of the trachea. For an ascending series of notes the larynx is raised, and the downward pull of the trachea increases in strength. Owing to the direction of the fibres the muscle mass of the vocal folds will be progressively pulled laterally, making the vibrating fold thinner.

The vocal muscle

The vocal muscle (vocalis muscle) can not be dissected into distinct anatomical parts; any partition or segmentation is purely functional (Mayet,

1955). The muscle fibres are arranged in rows behind one another. A small, inner portion of the muscle is embedded in the vocal cord (vocal ligament) (fig. 29). It consists of long fibres running parallel with the cord, *uninterruptedly*, from the angle of the thyroid cartilage to the vocal process of the arytenoid cartilage (Mayet, 1955). The main mass of the vocal muscle is situated deeper down in the larynx. One portion originates on the thyroid cartilage beneath the vocal cord, runs back laterally, and is attached to the muscular process of the arytenoid cartilage (fig. 28). This part is traversed by part of the lateral cricoarytenoid muscle (see fig. 32*a*), which starts at the conus elasticus and which also exerts a pull in the direction of the muscular process. As the pitch rises the vocal muscle is increasingly tensed. The lateral parts of the muscle, attached to the conus elasticus, will pull this aside under tension, and put themselves out of action (Negus, 1957). In

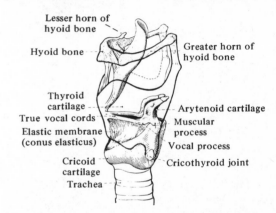

Fig. 28. The skeleton of the larynx. The thyroid cartilage is shown as though transparent. The hyoid bone is so firmly connected to the thyroid cartilage by means of tendons and muscles that functionally it may be regarded as belonging to the laryngeal skeleton. If the hand is put round the neck in a stranglehold, then the index finger and the thumb will touch the greater horns of the hyoid bone, which point backwards and serve as a point of attachment for the root of the tongue. The area between the fingers will rest against the body of the hyoid bone. The two large cartilages of the pharynx, the thyroid cartilage and the cricoid cartilage, are linked by joints. On the upper edge of the 'signet plate' of the cricoid cartilage the two small movable arytenoid cartilages ride, attached by strong ligaments. The vocal cords are the fortified upper edge of the elastic membrane (conus elasticus) with which the inside of the larynx is lined. They are stretched between the angle of the thyroid cartilage and the arytenoid cartilages. (After Benninghoff-Goerttler, 1967.)

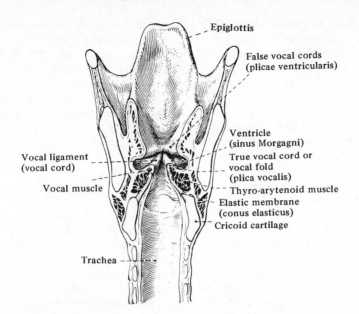

- Epiglottis
- False vocal cords (plicae ventricularis)
- Ventricle (sinus Morgagni)
- True vocal cord or vocal fold (plica vocalis)
- Thyro-arytenoid muscle
- Elastic membrane (conus elasticus)
- Cricoid cartilage
- Vocal ligament (vocal cord)
- Vocal muscle
- Trachea

Fig. 29. The interior of the larynx, seen from behind in frontal cross-section. There are two pairs of folds in the larynx, separated by a space known as the ventricle (sinus Morgagni). The uppermost folds are the *false* vocal cords (plicae ventricularis), while the lower are the *true* vocal cords (plicae vocalis), or more correctly the vocal *folds*. The true vocal folds may be defined as the vocal cords (vocal ligaments, the hard connective tissue margin of the vocal folds) and the muscular tissue of the vocal fold together with the elastic membrane (conus elasticus). (After Benninghoff-Goerttler, 1967.)

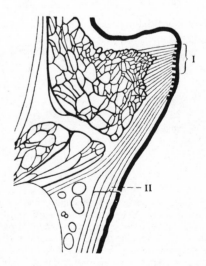

Fig. 31. Frontal cross-section of the left vocal fold, showing the direction of the fibres of connective tissue in the vocal cord (vocal ligament) (I) and in the conus elasticus (II). (After Mayet, 1955.)

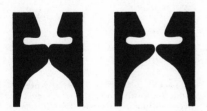

Fig. 30. The vocal folds when singing a high note (right) and a low note (left). (After Fritzell, 1973.)

51

this process the downward pull of the trachea is the main factor. In the head register only the middle, longitudinal portion of the vocal muscle vibrates.

The larynx in singing and swallowing

How can a singer ensure that the larynx assumes a relatively low position in all registers, with relatively relaxed vocal folds? In addition to yawning and covering the tone, he must avoid actively drawing the larynx up, which is what happens during swallowing. All the muscles involved in swallowing are centred on the hyoid bone. They comprise those shown in fig. 33 plus the hyoglossus muscle, which originates from the greater horns of the hyoid bone and is attached to the side of the tongue. When swallowing, these muscles cause the cartilages of the larynx to lock together; the entire larynx is then pulled upwards maximally and forwards. Meanwhile the epiglottis closes the entrance to the larynx. Compare fig. 33 with fig. 18a (p. 30), where the external muscles of the larynx are marked, most of which prepare the glottis for resonance and influence the pitch of the note. It can be seen that swallowing and singing are diametrically opposed laryngeal functions, and that finely controlled voluntary muscle movements are impossible during the swallowing reflex.[11]

Compensatory articulation

Compensatory articulation (p. 18) is presumed to be the result of the shaping of the vocal tract by the stylohyoid muscle (a swallowing muscle) remaining relaxed while the styloglossus and stylopharyngeal muscles are actively tensed. This occurs during the articulation of [ɩ] and [ɛ]. (For [ə] only the stylopharyngeal muscle is tensed.)

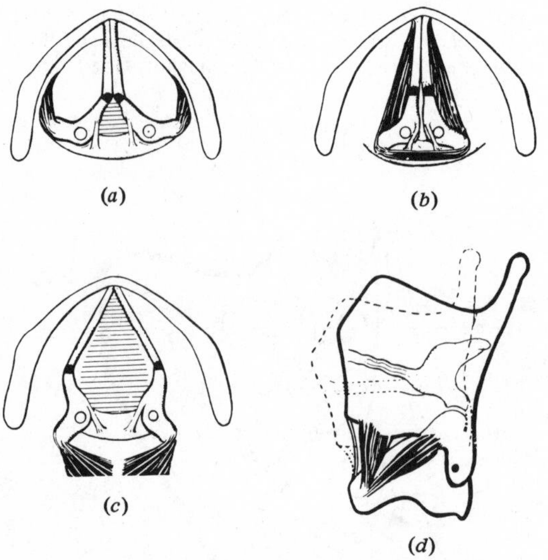

Appendix 4. Breathing

The exchange of oxygen and carbon dioxide in the blood takes place in the lungs, and depends on a constant replacement of air, i.e. breathing.

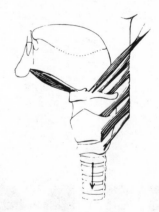

Fig. 32. Mechanisms in the larynx and glottis. (a) When the vocal cords (vocal ligaments) are closed only by the lateral cricoarytenoid muscle, there remains at the back of the glottis an opening that allows a whisper. (b) When the glottis is entirely closed to vocal sounds, the vocal muscle and the transverse arytenoid muscle are also activated. (c) When the glottis is wide open for inhalation the posterior cricoarytenoid muscle is activated. (d) With passive stretching of the vocal cords the thyroid cartilage nods forwards when the cricothyroid muscle is tensed. (After Benninghoff-Goerttler, 1967.)

Fig. 33. The muscles involved in swallowing. (After Benninghoff-Goerttler, 1967.)

11 When the act of swallowing is partially present during the production of the tone, the timbre will be thick and stiff, resulting in a throaty voice (German *Knödel*). The mutual movement of the laryngeal cartilages will be restricted: the larynx is drawn back/ up or (according to Martienssen-Lohman, 1956) down, when the alto tries to achieve an artificially dark-timbred voice.

Breathing is regulated via a centre in the brain, which monitors the oxygen and carbon dioxide concentrations of the blood and regulates the depth and frequency of breathing accordingly.

Normal inhalation and exhalation

During normal inhalation the external intercostal muscles (fig. 2) and the diaphragm are tensed, while the rectus muscle in the abdominal wall is relaxed. This causes an increase in the volume of the thorax and thus of the lungs. This increase in volume in turn causes a decrease in the air pressure in the lungs and so air flows in. This is accompanied by a straightening of the vertebral column (fig. 34), most noticeably in its upper portion, to give an 'inhalatory poise'.

Normal exhalation is largely passive. The breathing muscles are relaxed, the volume of the thorax and thus of the lungs is reduced, and so air flows out. The muscles in the abdominal wall are tensed by reflex (Benninghoff-Goerttler, 1968, p. 238), pushing the viscera (contents of the abdominal cavity) against the yielding diaphragm, which once again assumes a dome shape beneath the thorax. The tensing of the rectus muscle of the abdominal wall will, due to its vertical position, pull down the front of the thorax and the vertebral column yields. The result is an 'exhalatory poise'. In other words, normal breathing entails changes in poise.

The dorsal method of breathing

The dorsal method of breathing demands a characteristic poise, 'the singing posture' (fig. 8*a* and *c*), which releases the vertebral column. Inhalation takes place by means of a 'yawn', *without at the same time drawing breath*. Yawning involves tension of the upper pharyngeal constrictor (the 'yawn muscle'), releasing a powerful reflex tension of the diaphragm (Corda, von Euler and Lennerstrand, 1965; Takagi, Irwin and Bosma, 1966). The dome of the diaphragm is thus lowered and air streams in. Exhalation takes place in the ordinary way when the upper pharyngeal constrictor is relaxed. It must be pointed out that the secret of breath control during singing is to be able to maintain the inhalatory position (by activation of the upper pharynx) while at the same time flattening the thorax and supporting with the abdominal wall, thus creating a controlled, just sufficient, outgoing stream of air.

The membrane lining the pharynx, larynx, trachea and bronchi (fig. 16) is the site of initiation of reflex-like reactions during breathing. These reactions are inhalatory or exhalatory according to whether they emanate from the upper pharynx or from regions near the larynx. From the upper pharynx the inhalatory muscles are tensed and the bronchi (and even blood vessels of the body) caused to expand. From the lower pharynx and the larynx the abdominal wall, which is the actual exhalatory muscle system, is tensed, and bronchi

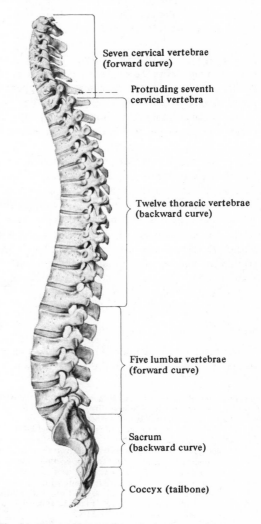

Seven cervical vertebrae (forward curve)

Protruding seventh cervical vertebra

Twelve thoracic vertebrae (backward curve)

Five lumbar vertebrae (forward curve)

Sacrum (backward curve)

Coccyx (tailbone)

Fig. 34. Curvatures of the vertebral column. (After Benninghoff-Goerttler, 1968.)

53

and blood vessels are constricted (Tomori, Widdicombe and Chechoslov, 1969).[12] Breath control during singing is thus provided by *conscious* activation of the upper pharynx. At the same time the thorax is flattened and there is support by the abdominal wall, so that the net result is an outgoing stream of air.

The song-stretch

From the vertebral column impulses run to the intercostal muscles of the ribs. Moreover, close to the vertebral column there are short strips of muscle that initiate reflexes in the diaphragm (Decima, von Euler and Thoden, 1969); for this reason the song-*stretch* is important.

Ascending pitch   The inhalatory reflex is gradually set in motion as the song-stretch progresses. At the same time activity increases in the upper pharyngeal constrictor (increasing yawn), the thorax becomes more flattened (elliptical) in shape, and the air pressure in the lungs increases.

Descending pitch   Activity in the frontal portions of the upper pharyngeal constrictor decreases,[13] and the air pressure in the lungs is reduced. It is important, however, not to relax the tension in the *entire* upper pharyngeal constrictor, or the reflex actions will be lost and the singer left without breath. In the vertebral column the stretch can first be felt frontally in the cervical column, after which it becomes more marked in the lumbar regions.

Vowel formation

Vowel formation in the dorsal method takes place in the upper pharynx,[14] and the primary articulators of the vowel are the derivatives of the upper pharyngeal constrictor. These muscles extend along the entire length of the pharynx. When the back vowels [ɑ], [ɔ] and [u] are articulated, the levator muscle of the soft palate and the palatopharyngeal muscle are activated. The levator increases the volume of the rear part of the oral cavity; the palatopharyngeal muscle pulls the side walls of the pharynx closer to the central line (Benninghoff-Goerttler, 1967, p. 63). The pharynx is thus given a high, narrow shape. Broad vowels are given extra support by the muscles of the styloid process (fig. 18*b*). As the styloid process is ventral to the cervical vertebrae and lateral to the pharynx, these muscles will pull the head forwards and give the vocal tract a broad shape. The stylopharyngeal muscle alone will provide the lateral tension for the vowel [ə]. In addition, the styloglossus muscle is activated for the vowels [i] and [ɛ], so that the ridge of the tongue, too, broadens.

Appendix 5. Types of breathing

The diaphragm and the intercostal muscles of the ribs are always tensed simultaneously when inhaling, but certain types of breathing can best be understood on the basis of the movement of the ribs, while others are conceived as a movement of the diaphragm. Of the six types mentioned here, four are described as 'rib breathing' and two as 'diaphragmatic breathing' (see figs. 2, 3 and 4).

(1) *High costal* (see fig. 4). The vertebral muscles are tensed, the curvature in the thoracic vertebrae is straightened out, and the vertebrae 'sink into the thorax'. The upper part of the body leans back, and the rib-cage is lifted. The uppermost pair of ribs pulls the sternum (breastbone) up, and tips it forwards. This draws the 'true' ribs with it (fig. 4). The thoracic cavity is expanded in front to produce a 'high costal breath' (costal means 'of the ribs'), which belongs to the era of

12 Experience has shown that singing in accordance with the methods in which reflexes from upper and lower pharynx act alternately on the lungs, makes for improved mucus drainage and relieves bronchial asthma (Butenschøn, 1976).

13 Bosma states that not necessarily the *whole* of the palatopharyngeal muscle *and* the upper pharyngeal constrictor take part in phonation (Bosma and Fletcher, 1962), which is in agreement with Butenschøn's experience and observation. She claims that small adjustments of stretch lead to specific and nuanced activation of these muscles.

14 There is an account dating from about 1700 of a girl who was born without a tongue who was nevertheless able to talk. There have also been occasions when people have had their tongue cut out as a punishment. Nowadays certain diseases, such as cancer, sometimes involve removing the tongue muscle, in some cases right down to the root. Patients who have undergone an operation of this kind can nevertheless still talk; one man ran his own business, both by telephone and direct communication. There was no explanation of these phenomena until it was realised that the formation of vowels takes place in the upper pharynx (Bosma and Fletcher, 1962).

tight bodices: consequently this is a method of singing that has more or less been abandoned.

(2) *High costal and lateral.* The breathing is high costal but at the same time the 'true' ribs expand the rib-cage laterally.

(3) *More lateral.* Breathing is more lateral. Owing to the suspension and shaping of the ribs the lower opening of the thorax is expanded laterally.

(4) *Dorsal and lateral.* In man the vertebral column is set well in between the ribs (fig. 35*a*), which thus curve backwards before sweeping round to the front of the body. In this method of breathing the vertebral column is the point of attack from which inhalation starts, so the ribs are drawn back and at the same time further sideways, expanding the dorsal part of the thorax. This expansion is increased when the curvature of the lumbar regions is straightened. This type of breathing is used in the dorsal method, and should be combined with type (6).

(5) *'Breathing with the stomach'.* During inhalation the diaphragm is tensed, and lowered. The thorax is expanded at the expense of the abdominal cavity. 'Breathing with the stomach' (when standing) means that the side muscles of the abdominal wall (fig. 6, p. 10) pull the edge of the ribs down. There is an exaggerated forward bulge of the stomach. The method is recommended by doctors and physiotherapists in cases of over-tense abdominal muscles or exaggerated high costal breathing.

(6) *Edge of the ribs up.* The diaphragm rises vertically from its anchorage in the lateral part of the edge of the ribs (Campbell, 1958), and adheres firmly to the wall of the thorax. During inhalation the edge of the ribs is drawn up and pushed out laterally. The circumference of the thorax is expanded and thus the volume of the abdominal cavity increases more than the volume reduction caused by the lowering of the diaphragm (after Campbell, 1958, p. 36). The viscera are drawn to the sides, and the stomach is *not* pushed forward. Breathing is lateral. This type of breathing is used concomitantly with type (4) in the dorsal singing method.

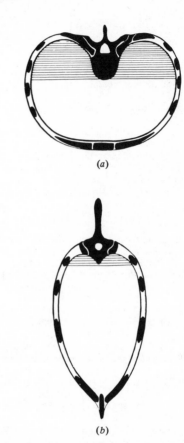

Fig. 35. Cross-section of the thorax in (*a*) a human being and (*b*) a dog. In the human being the vertebral column is depressed into the thoracic cavity in between the ribs. (After Benninghoff-Goerttler, 1968.)

Bibliography

Agostoni, E. & Magnoni, B. (1966). Deformation of the chest wall during breathing efforts. *J. Appl. Physiol.* **21**, 1827–32.

Alvik, I. (1953). *Generell ortopedisk kirurgi.* Olaf Norlis forlag, Oslo.

Andrew, B.L. (1955). The respiratory displacement of the larynx. *J. Physiol.* **130**, 473–85.

Barnicol, A. (1953). See Minnigerode (1967).

Benninghoff-Goerttler, O. (1967). *Lehrbuch der Anatomie des Menschen*, 8th edn.
(1968). *Lehrbuch der Anatomie des Menschen*, 10th edn.

Bosma, J.F. (1957). Deglution, Pharyngeal stage. *Physiol. Rev.* **37**, 275–300.
(1963). Oral and pharyngeal development and function. *J. Dent. Res.* **42**, Suppl. 2, 375–80.

Bosma, J.F. & Fletcher, S.G. (1962). The upper pharynx. II. *Ann. Otol. Rhinol. Laryngol.* **72**, 135–51.

Brauss, H. (1929–40). *Anatomie des Menschen*, vol. 2, p. 80.

Brodal, A. (1952). *Vår hjerne.* Tanum, Oslo.

Buchtahl, F. & Faaborg-Andersen, K. (1964). *Ann. Otol. Rhinol. Laryngol.* **73**, 118–23.

Butenschøn, S. (1976). *Sang som middel til selvdrenasje ved bronchialastma.* Norsk Mensendieckforbund no. 3.

Campbell, E.J.M. (1958). *The Respiratory Muscles and the Mechanics of Breathing.* London.
(1970). *Hering-Breuer Centenary Symposium. Ciba Foundation*, p. 173.

Corda, M., von Euler, C. & Lennerstrand, G. (1965). Proprioceptive innervation of the diaphragm. *J. Physiol.* **178**, 161–77.

Decima, E.E., von Euler, C. & Thoden, U. (1969). Intercostal to phrenic reflexes in the spinal cat. I. *Acta Physiol. Scand.* **75**, 568–97.

Faaborg-Andersen, K. & Sonninen, A. (1960). The function of the extrinsic laryngeal muscles at different pitch. *Acta Otolaryngol.* **51**, 89–93.

Faaborg-Andersen, K. & Vennard, W. (1964). Electromyography of extrinsic muscles during phonation of different vowels. *Ann. Otol. Rhinol. Laryngal.* **73**, 248–54.

Fant, G. (1960). *Acoustic Theory of Speech Production: X-ray Studies of Russian Articulation.* Stockholm.

Flach, M. & Schwickardi, H. (1966). Die Recessus Piriformis unter phoniatrischer Sicht. *Fol. Phoniatr.* **18**, 153–64.

Floyd, W.F., Negus, V.E. & Neil, E. (1957). Observations on the mechanism of phonation. *Acta Otolaryngol.* **48**, 16–25.

Fritzell, B. (1973). *Foniatri för medicinare.* Almquist & Wiksell, Stockholm.

Gardiner, J. (1968). *A Guide to Good Singing and Speech.* Cassell, London.

Gaukstad, Ø. (1962). *Musikkleksikon.* Oslo.

Gelder, L. van (1965). *Het zachte Gehemmelte bij de Spraak.* Harlem.

Gribbe, P.O. (1956). Wenner-Grens Institut, Stockholm. Personal communication. (1965).

Husler, F. & Rodd-Marling, Y. (1956). *Singing, the Physical Nature of the Vocal Organ.* London.

Kotby, M., Nasser, O. & Haugen, L.K. (1970). The mechanics of laryngeal function. *Acta Otolaryngol.* **70**, 203–11.

Leanderson, R. (1972). On the functional organisation of facial muscles in speech. *Acta Otolaryngol.* 11pp.

Lindblom, B. (1963). Spectrographic study of vowel reduction. *J. Acoust. Soc. Am.* **35**, 1773–80.

Luchsinger, R. (1950). Schalldruck und Geschwindigkeitsregistrierung der Atemluft beim Singen. *Int. Ass. Logoph. Phoniatr.* **8**, 42–65.

Luchsinger, R. & Arnold, G.E. (1959). *Lehrbuch der Stimm- und Sprachheilkunde.* Vienna.

Malmberg, B. (1968). *Manual of Phonetics.* North-Holland, Amsterdam.

Martienssen Lohman, E. (1956). *Der wissende Sänger.* Zurich.

Mayet, A. (1955). Zur funktionellen Anatomie der menschlichen Stimmlippe. *Z. Anat. Entwicklungsgesch.* **119**, 87–111.

Minnigerode, B. (1967). Bedeutung der extralaryngealen Muskulatur. *Arch. klin. Exp. Ohren-Nasen-Kehlkopfheilk.* **188**, 603–25.

Monnier, M. (1970). *Functions of the Nervous System*, vol. 2.

Nail, B.S., Sterling, G.M. & Widdicombe, J.G. (1969). Epipharyngeal receptors responding to mechanical stimulation. *J. Physiol.* **204**, 91–8.

Negus, V.E. (1929). *Mechanism of the Larynx.* London.
(1949). *Comparative Anatomy of the Larynx.* London.
(1957). Mechanism of the larynx. *Laryngoscope.* **67**, 961–86.

Ringel, R.L., Saxman, J.H. & Brooks, A.R. (1967). Oral perception. II. Mandibular kinestesia. *JSHR* **10**, 639–42.

Rubin, H.J. & Hirt, Ch.C. (1960). The falsetto. A high-speed cinematographic study. *Laryngoscope* **70**, 1305–24.

Rubin, H.J., Le Cover, M. & Vennard, W. (1967). Vocal intensity, subglottic pressure and air flow relationships in singers. *Fol. Phoniatr.* **19**, 393–410.

Selmer, E.W. & Broch, O. (1950). *Håndbok i elementær fonetikk*, 5th edn.

Sercer, A. (1962). La marche bipède, la phonation et la parole. *Rev. Laryngol. Otol. Rhinol.* **83**.

Shelton, R.L. & Bosma, J.F. (1962) Maintenance of the pharyngeal airway. *J. Appl. Physiol.* **17**, 209–14.

Sokolowsky, R.R. (1943). Effect of the extrinsic laryngeal muscles on voice production. *Arch. Otolaryngol.* **38**.

Sonninen, Aa. (1956). The external laryngeal muscles in length-adjustment of the vocal cords in singing. *Acta Otolaryngol., Suppl.* **130**, 96pp.

(1962). Paratasisgram of the vocal cords and the dimensions of the voice. In *Proceedings of the IVth International Congress on Phonetic Science,* *Helsinki*, pp. 252–8.

(1968). The external frame function in the control of pitch in the human voice. *N.Y. Acad. Sci.* **155**, 68–89.

Stevens, K.N. & House, A.S. (1972). In *Speech Perception in Foundations of Modern Auditory Theory*, ed. J.V. Tobias, vol. 2, pp. 1–57. Academic Press, New York & London.

Takagi, Y., Irwin, J.V. & Bosma, J.F. (1966). Effect of stimulations of pharynx on respiration. *J. Appl. Physiol.* **21**, 454–62.

Tomori, Z., Widdicombe, J.G. & Chechoslov, O. (1969). Muscular, bronchomotor and cardiovascular reflexes elicited by mechanical stimulation of the respiratory tract. *J. Physiol.* **200**, 25–49.

Wustlow, F. (1952). Bau und Funktion des menschlichen musculus vocalis. *Z. Anat. Entwicklungsgesch.* 116pp.

Wyss, O.A.M. (1964). Die nervöse Steuerung der Atmung. *Ergebn. Physiol.* **54**, 1–479.

Index and glossary

dorsal   at or near the back of the body (cf. ventral)

ellipsoid   the shape of an ellipse. The area of an ellipse is smaller than that of a circle with the same circumference. 'Flattening the thorax' (making it more ellipsoid) reduces its volume and makes air flow out (exhalation). See p. 5

epigastrium   the upper middle part of the abdomen

epiglottis   lid-like structure that covers the entrance to the larynx during swallowing. See fig. 29, p. 51

euphonious   sounding pleasant, harmonious

Eustachian tube   canal between the middle ear and the upper pharynx. See fig. 27, p. 49

exhalation   flow of air out of the lungs

exhalatory poise   poise resulting from exhalation, the thorax being pulled down in front by the rectus muscle. See p. 53

false ribs   fig. 4, p. 6

false vocal cords   fig. 29, p. 51

falsetto   p. 32

femur   the thigh bone

floating ribs   fig. 4, p. 6

formants   groups of strong harmonics (overtones higher than the fundamental note) in speech sounds, created by resonance in the cavities of the mouth, pharynx and larynx. The distribution patterns of formants are different in characteristic for each phoneme (its 'timbre'). See p. 17

forte   high volume; abbr. *f*

frequency (of a sound)   vibrations per second. *See also* c.p.s.

frontal   at or near the front/abdominal side of the body

front vowels   the vowels [i], [ɛ] and [e] (as in m*a*de)

full-bodied timbre   ex. 8, p. 12

fundamental note   most often the (lowest) perceived pitch of a complex note, the pitch corresponding to the frequency of vibration of the vocal folds (glottis note)

glissando   sliding continuously from one note to another, including all the intermediate frequencies

glottis   the opening between the vocal cords. Often used to denote the vocal folds with surrounding structures. See fig. 32, p. 52

glottis note   *see* fundamental note

grace notes   notes added for embellishment, usually printed as small notes just before the note they embellish and from which their time value is subtracted. See pp. 44–5

hamulus   fig. 5, p. 7; fig. 27, p. 49

head register   p. 32; ex. 38, p. 36

homogenous   smooth, of the same kind

humerus   the bone of the upper arm

humming   singing with the mouth closed, without vowels. See pp. 9–10

hyoid bone   fig. 28, p. 50

hypothesis   supposition or theory assumed for the sake of argument to be correct until proved otherwise

iliac crest   fig. 22, p. 35

inguinal ligament   fig. 22, p. 35

inhalation   air flow into the lungs

inhalatory poise   poise resulting from inhalation, that is straightening the upper part of the vertebral column. See p. 53

intensity   here: tone volume

interval   the distance, or difference in pitch, between two notes

ischial tuberosity   fig. 7, p. 11

isometric   of equal measure or length. The isometric contraction of a muscle means that the muscle is *tensed but not shortened*, because counteracting muscles, or pressure against fixed structures (e.g. a wall) prevents movement and shortening

jaw
    anatomy of   fig. 13(*a*), p. 23
    muscles of   fig. 10, p. 19
    opening of   fig. 13, p. 23; table 2, p. 25; p. 31

Knödel   n. 11, p. 52

larynx   pp. 49–52
    positions of   p. 17; fig. 17, p. 29; fig. 20, p. 33

lateral   at or near the side

'leaking tone'   excess air escaping through the glottis during phonation; 'exhalation while singing'

legato   performance of a melodic sequence in a smooth, gliding manner without soundless pauses between the notes, changing rapidly from one pitch to another (no *glissando*)

lips (positions of in singing)   table 2, p. 25

lumbar   at or near the 'small' of the back

lumbar vertebrae   fig. 4, p. 6; fig. 34, p. 53

mastoid process   ex. 2, p. 7; fig. 10, p. 19

methods of singing   table 2, p. 25

mezzo   (the range of) the middle female voice, deeper than soprano and higher than alto

modulate   (1) to adjust to something; (2) to shift to another key; (3) to vary the pitch and/or intensity of the voice

mucous membrane   membrane lubricated by mucus, such as forms the inner lining of the respiratory system

muscles
    abdominal   fig. 6, p. 10; fig. 9, p. 15; fig. 24, p. 38
    of cervical region   fig. 21, p. 34
    chondroglossus   fig. 28, p. 50; p. 32
    constrictors of pharynx   fig. 26, p. 48; fig. 27, p. 49; fig. 33, p. 52
    cricoarytenoid   fig. 32(*a*) and (*c*), p. 52
    cricothyroid   fig. 32(*d*), p. 52
    depressor anguli oris   fig. 14, p. 24
    erector spinae   fig. 7, p. 11; fig. 11(*a*), p. 21
    gluteus maximus   fig. 8(*c*), p. 14
    hyoglossus   fig. 15, p. 25
    iliocostalis   fig. 11(*a*), p. 21
    iliopsoas   fig. 22, p. 35
    intercostales, external   fig. 9, p. 15

sphincter muscle   a muscle surrounding, and able to shut, an orifice: e.g. in the anus

spinous process   the vertebral processes that point backwards and can be felt as hard 'lumps' along the vertebral column (spine)

staccato   a melodic sequence performed with notes of short duration and soundless intervals (pauses) between the notes (opposite: *legato*)

sternum   the breastbone

stressed vowels   p. 3; pp. 42–4

styloid process   fig. 10, p. 19; fig. 18(*b*), p. 31

support area   ex. 6, p. 9; fig. 6, p. 10

swallowing   p. 52

synergist   a muscle aiding the effect of another muscle

thoracic vertebrae   fig. 34, p. 53

thorax   the chest cage

   shape of when singing   ex. 20, p. 20

throaty voice   n. 11, p. 52

thyroid cartilage   fig. 16, p. 28

timbre   the quality or 'colour' of sound given by the (characteristic) pattern of harmonics (overtones) that are created by resonance in the sounding instrument or voice

tone   a vocal or musical sound

   'falling from the resonance cavity'   ex. 12, p. 12

   leaking   air escaping through the glottis during phonation

tone quality   *see* timbre

tongue   fig. 25, p. 39

trachea   the windpipe

transition   a passing from one condition to another. Here, from one vocal register to another

trill   a rapid alternation of two musical tones one note or half a note apart. See p. 44

unstressed vowels   p. 3; pp. 42–4

uvula   fig. 5, p. 7

ventral   at or near the front of the body

ventricle   a cavity

ventricle of larynx   sinus Morgagni: the cavity between the false and the true vocal cords. See fig. 29, p. 51

vertebral column   the backbone. See fig. 34, p. 53

vestigial   of the nature of a trace or relic

viscera   the contents of the abdominal cavity

vocal cord   anatomically the vocal ligament, which is the connective tissue margin of the vocal fold. In less precise, non-scientific language vocal cord is often used as a synonym for vocal fold. See n. 1, p. 4 and fig. 29, p. 51

vocal fold   anatomically the vocal ligament plus vocalis muscle plus conus elasticus plus the mucous membrane lining the interior of the larynx. See n. 1, p. 4 and fig. 29, p. 51

vocal process (of arytenoid cartilage)   fig. 28, p. 50

vocal tract   the region from the glottis to the lips and nostrils

vocalise   to sing a chain of vowels, either in random order or by omitting the consonants when singing the lyrics of a song

Vollton   full-bodied, rich timbre; superior tone quality

volume   intensity of tone, fullness of tone/voice

vowel(s)

   back   the vowels [a] and [ɔ]

   front   the vowels [i], [ɛ] and [e] (as in m*a*de)

   stressed   p. 3; pp. 42–4

   unstressed   p. 3; pp. 42–4

   'jumping into the mouth'   ex. 27 (mistake), p. 26

   'swallowing itself'   p. 31

yawn   used in this book/song method to assure proper breath control (*see* breath control) and a low position of the larynx while singing. See p. 49

yawn muscle   the upper pharyngeal constrictor. See fig. 26, p. 48; fig. 27, p. 49

yawn/stretch   pp. 4–5; pp. 7–8